# How to WIN at College

# How to WIN at College

### at College

*Surprising Secrets for Success
from the Country's Top Students*

**CAL NEWPORT**

THREE RIVERS PRESS

NEW YORK

Published in the United States by Three Rivers Press, an
imprint of the Crown Publishing Group, a division of
Random House, Inc., New York.

Originally published in the United States by Broadway
Books, an imprint of the Broadway Doubleday
Publishing Group, a division of Random House, Inc.,
New York, in 2005.

Three Rivers Press and the Tugboat design are
registered trademarks of Random House, Inc.

Printed in the United States of America

Visit our website at www.threeriverspress.com

*Book design by Michael Collica*

Library of Congress Cataloging-in-Publication Data
Newport, Cal.
    How to win at college : surprising secrets for
success from the country's top students / Cal
Newport.
        p.   cm.
    ISBN 0-7679-1787-1 (alk. paper)
    1. College student orientation.   I. Title.
LB2343.3.N49    2005
378.1'98—dc22

                                        2004051886

30 29 28 27 26 25 24 23 22

First Three Rivers Press Edition

# Contents

*Introduction*                                                                1

1   Don't Do All of Your Reading                                              7

2   Create a Sunday Ritual                                                   10

3   Drop Classes Every Semester                                             12

4   Start Long-Term Projects the Day They Are Assigned                       14

5   Make Your Bed                                                            16

6   Apply to Ten Scholarships a Year                                         18

7   Build Study Systems                                                      20

8   Befriend a Professor                                                     22

9   Become a Club President                                                  25

10  Read a Newspaper Every Day                                               27

11  Do One Thing Better Than Anyone Else You Know                            29

12  Avoid Daily To-Do Lists                                                  32

13  Learn to Give Up                                                         35

14  Never Nap                                                                39

15    Sign Up for Something Your First Week    41

16    Always Be Working on a "Grand Project"    43

17    Take Art History and Astronomy    46

18    Blow the Curve Once a Term    49

19    Ask One Question at Every Lecture    51

20    Jump into Research as Soon as Possible    53

21    Pay Your Dues    56

22    Study in Fifty-Minute Chunks    58

23    Schedule Your Free Time    60

24    Dress Nicely for Class    63

25    Decorate Your Room    65

26    Start Studying Two Weeks in Advance    68

27    Write Outside of Class    71

28    Eat Alone Twice a Day    73

29    Find an Escape    75

30    Take Hard Courses Early On    77

31    Don't Study in Your Room    79

32    Don't Study in Groups    81

33    Join an Honors Program    83

34    Do Schoolwork Every Day    85

35    Attend Guest Lectures    87

36    Exercise Five Days a Week    89

37    Stay in Touch    91

38    Tack on an Extra Major or Minor    93

39    Meet Often with Your Adviser    96

40    Don't Get a Normal Job    98

41    Use Three Days to Write a Paper    101

42    Don't Undersleep, Don't Oversleep    105

43 Relax Before Exams 107

44 Make Friends Your #1 Priority 110

45 Don't Binge Drink 112

46 Ignore Your Classmates' Grades 114

47 Seek Out Phenomenal Achievers 116

48 Learn to Listen 119

49 Never Pull an All-Nighter 122

50 Laugh Every Day 125

51 Use High-Quality Notebooks 127

52 Keep a Work-Progress Journal 129

53 Seek Out Fun 132

54 Inflate Your Ambition 134

55 Get Involved with Your Major Department 136

56 Care About Your Grades, Ignore Your G.P.A. 138

57 Always Go to Class 141

58 Set Arbitrary Deadlines 143

59 Eat Healthy 145

60 Volunteer Quietly 147

61 Write as if Going for a Pulitzer 149

62 Attend Political Rallies 152

63 Maximize Your Summers 154

64 Choose Goals, Explore Routes 158

65 Don't Take Breaks Between Classes 161

66 Don't Network 164

67 Publish Op-Eds 168

68 Use a Filing Cabinet 170

69 Find a Secret Study Space 172

70 Study with the Quiz-and-Recall Method 175

CONTENTS

71  Empty Your In-Box                          179

72  Relax Before Sleep                         181

73  Start Fast, End Slow                       183

74  Spend a Semester Studying Abroad           185

75  "Don't Have No Regrets"                    188

viii

# How to WIN at College

## Introduction

*College. You've probably* been hearing about it and planning for it for years, and now, it's finally here. The SATs are over, your application's been accepted, and high school is soon to become just another fading memory. You're about to embark on a great adventure—one you'll remember your entire life.

There is no question that college is a lot of fun. It's four years of freedom and excitement and growth. Staying out until two A.M. partying, and staying up until dawn talking with friends. Reveling in the chaos of cramming for midterms, and discovering how to appreciate dining hall food. Learning how to write a powerful, persuasive paper, and figuring out how to transform your bedsheet into a toga. Trust me when I say that you're in for a good time.

However, there is more to four years of college than amusement. It's also the launching pad for the rest of your life. The tough truth is that getting a good job these days is hard. Getting accepted to a good law school, graduate school, or medical school is also hard. You have just four short years to prepare yourself for the world beyond your college campus. If you play your cards right, you will have the ability to engage in any pursuit that inspires you. If you don't make the most of these four years, getting started on an exciting and fulfilling life path will be much more difficult.

Is it possible to be successful at college and still have fun? When I first arrived at school, I didn't think so. I thought there was no way that you could both enjoy college life and excel as a student. As I saw it, there were two choices: you could be fun and social and put all your energy into meeting people and having memorable experiences, or you could be a grind, and while away your weekend hours studying in the depths of the library. I truly didn't believe you could do both. Until, that is, I met Heidi.

Everyone liked Heidi. She was fun and outgoing, she knew tons of people, and she seemed to exude energy. It was clear that she was having a good time at college. But here's the catch: she was also a Rhodes Scholar. Not to mention a published author in the field of mathematics, a winner of a National Science Foundation Graduate Research Fellowship, and the founder of a successful community service organization for young girls.

I also met Kabir. He was a fun-loving member of a fraternity I frequented, a musician in a popular campus jazz group, and an all-around sociable guy. However, when I really got to know him, I discovered that he was also the CEO of a start-up company, a cofounder of a grassroots mentoring program in Australia, and a rising star in the world of youth politics.

Then there was Janos, who, in a brilliant display of social vitality, somehow managed to become a member of both a fraternity and a co-ed social house—a definite fixture on the campus party scene. But this whirlwind social life didn't stop him from serving as student body president two years in a row, nor did it stop him from planning a postgraduation run for the state assembly.

Clearly, these students were proof that academic success and real-world ambitions could go hand in hand with living college life to the fullest. They seemed bounded by nothing. After they graduated, the most competitive companies would hire them, the most exclusive academic programs would admit them, and the most important people would love to meet them. They had, however, avoided the fate of those tedious students who spend their college years in a tireless pursuit of a perfect G.P.A. Instead, they were having a great time, building friendships, and all the while managing to rack up incredibly impressive achievements that would serve them well down the line. None of these students was interested in achieving solely for achieving's sake; rather, they had a natural hunger for intellectual challenge and a flair for transforming their personal interests into exciting projects. Their experiences convinced me that becoming a standout student was not only the best way to prepare for life in the real world, it was also the best way to make college memorable and fulfilling.

This is what inspired me to write this book: I wanted to find out how to be like Heidi, Kabir, or Janos. In search of these answers, I frequented the "College Life" section of quite a few bookstores, but came up frustratingly empty-handed. There were plenty of campus guides, books full of practical financial-aid information, and tutorials on how to score high on the SATs, write smart application essays, and other tricks for getting into good schools. There were books that professed to help you learn to speed-read, develop a super-sharp memory, and improve your study skills. And there were plenty of titles brimming with practical advice for surviving college—from how to do your laundry to how to avoid the "freshmen fifteen." But there were no books about how to achieve the head-turning, interesting, and rewarding college experiences boasted by students like Heidi, Kabir, and Janos. I wanted real advice on how to do the exceptional things they were doing.

Because I couldn't find the answers I wanted at the bookstore, I went searching for them myself. I began to track down and interview top students across the country—not just the academic stars, but students who fully embodied this unique brand of multifaceted success. From the Ivy League—Harvard, Princeton, Yale, Dartmouth, and Cornell—to Stanford, Kansas State, Wake Forest, Clemson, the University of Wyoming, the University of Virginia, and the University of Arizona, I located some incredible students, and I asked them about the habits, systems, and mind-sets that had aided them in their accomplishments. I had them write to-do lists for incoming college freshmen interested in doing well at college, and I pressed them for details about specific approaches to time management, studying, and balancing a social life with working hard. Essentially, I wanted to find out everything that made these superstars tick.

To be honest, when I first started these interviews, I was a little intimidated. I worried that I would discover that the key to winning at college was a genius-level I.Q., an ability to go for days without sleep, or maybe even a photographic memory. But my fears were unfounded. I discovered from my research that **anyone can become a standout student!** You don't have to be a genius, you are allowed to get a healthy amount of sleep, and your memory doesn't have to be anything special. All you really need is some expert guidance from those who have done it before.

How should you prepare for exams and papers? What extracurricular opportunities should you look into? How should you deal with professors? What's the best way to keep your intellect stimulated and your mood upbeat? How do you balance a fun social life with an ambitious schedule? And how can you craft your pursuits to perfectly fit *your* abilities, interests, and passions? These are the important questions that every student needs to ask. And *How to Win at College* contains the answers.

In this book you'll find seventy-five rules drawn from the experiences of some of the country's most phenomenal students. Their answers cover the questions asked above, and more. Turn to any page and you will encounter a simple piece of advice to help you make the most of your four years. No one chapter will turn you into a Rhodes Scholar, and you certainly don't need to follow all

5

seventy-five. However, if you select a group of rules that really captures your attention, and then take the time to implement them in your everyday college life, you will notice remarkable results. Half the battle in becoming a standout student—in fact, to becoming a standout individual—is making the decision to actively try to succeed. If you follow the advice in this book, you will be well on your way toward taking advantage of all that college has to offer, and ensuring yourself the strongest possible start in the real world that follows. *How to Win at College* will help you find that perfect balance needed to jump-start a life filled with interesting enthusiasms, impressive achievements, and wonderful acquaintances and friends.

6          I wish you the best of luck with this exciting new phase. Hopefully, this book will help you meet and master the many opportunities that will come your way.

—Cal Newport

# 1

## Don't Do All of Your Reading

*You will be* assigned a lot of reading at college. Probably more reading than seems humanly possible for any one person to complete. Social science and humanities courses will taunt you with seemingly short academic articles that turn out to be riddled with Byzantine sentence structures and devilishly complicated logic. Science courses will siphon your time, and help you develop a life-long hatred of bar charts, with a steady stream of ultradense technical material. And just to keep things sporting, professors will periodically slip entire books into the syllabus, often giving you only a week or so to finish them. Sound bleak? It doesn't have to be. All you need remember is one simple rule: **Don't do all of your reading.**

To a hardworking student, ignoring assigned reading probably seems blasphemous. But as unusual as this may sound at first, covering every page of reading listed in a course syllabus is rarely necessary. Here is what you should do instead:

For reading that covers the topic of an upcoming lecture, it's often sufficient to just skim the main points ahead of time, and then fill in the gaps during class by taking very good notes. Students are sometimes afraid of skimming, but you shouldn't be. You need to master the skill of covering hundreds of pages of text very quickly. The secret is to read chapter introductions and conclusions carefully, and then skim everything else. Make tick marks next to sentences that catch your attention—this is faster than highlighting. Don't get bogged down trying to understand the significance of every paragraph. Instead, note only the passages that seem to obviously support the thesis. You will definitely miss some key points, but your professor won't. So pay attention in class when the work is discussed, and you will pick up the arguments that you overlooked. Come exam time, your lecture notes, plus a review of the sentences you marked, will bring you up to speed on the material.

If there is a particular assignment that was not covered in class, but you know that it will be part of an upcoming exam, skim over it more carefully. If you still feel shaky on the topic, go to office hours. Discuss with your professor the conclusions of the reading. Take good notes. This combination of careful skimming and a good record of the professor's thoughts on what's important is a very effective way to prepare material for testing.

When multiple books are assigned as background for a paper, find out early exactly what your paper topic will be, and read

8

only the material you need to develop your specific thesis. Skip optional readings. With all due respect to your professors, there are better uses for your limited time.

For science courses, you will typically be assigned one or two chapters of dense technical material to review for each class. These assignments almost always cover the exact same topics that the professor will detail in lecture. Skim these chapters quickly so you know what to expect, but put the bulk of your energy into concentrating in class. Sciences courses don't test you on your reading. They test you on the concepts taught in the classroom. Your goal as a science student should be to come away from each lecture understanding what was covered, and feel comfortable about applying it. If you find yourself falling behind the professor's chalkboard heroics, ramp up the amount of preparatory reading you are doing until you are able to comfortably follow along. In general, reading in science courses should consume very little of your time. Put your attention where it matters: class lectures and homework problems.

This approach to completing class work is admittedly an acquired skill. At first you should err on the side of caution, doing as much reading as possible. But as you gain a feel for your professors, and the structure of your courses, you can begin to back off on your assigned reading until you find that perfect balance between being prepared and being efficient. If you have ever wondered how top students can accomplish so much work in such limited amounts of time, this rule is a large part of the answer.

9

# 2

## Create a Sunday Ritual

*For an ambitious* college student, Sunday is the most important day of the week. Even though it's tempting on a Sunday morning to just curl up on your couch and become intimately reacquainted with your old friend the TV, you really must resist. Why? Because **Sunday sets the tone for the week that follows.**

This is absolutely true. If you attack the day on Sunday, you will start your week with momentum behind you. If you let the day attack you, your week will quickly devolve into one protracted game of catch-up. So how do you overcome the allure of lounging and make your Sundays count? The secret is to engage in the same focusing ritual every Sunday morning—something that wakes up your mind and gets your day moving. Read the paper with a strong cup of coffee, take a walk with a friend, go for a jog followed by a hot shower, or spend some time browsing in a nearby bookstore.

**CAL NEWPORT**

Then, with your intellectual energy piqued, and your focus strong, settle into a quiet spot at the library and start working. While other students slumber, you will have a full, undisturbed day to get ahead of your work obligations.

This weekend ritual will also help you make that vital mental switch from weekend debauchery to workweek focus. When you party straight through the weekend until Sunday night, Monday morning is all the more depressing. The satisfaction you'll get from starting the week in full command of your responsibilities will provide the good mood and momentum needed to get through the days that follow. If you take control of your Sunday, you take control of your week.

# 3

## Drop Classes Every Semester

*If you are* a collegiate superman, then bad courses are your kryptonite. You should never underestimate the importance of picking a winning schedule every single semester. Good courses, with engaging professors and reasonable requirements, are the key to a great educational experience. Bad courses, with incompatible professors and unreasonable requirements, are the key to developing an ulcer. **You must avoid bad courses at all costs.** They will make you unhappy, they will upset your academic momentum, they will sap your will to achieve, and they will hurt your grades.

So how do you keep your schedule solid one hundred percent of the time? Take advantage of the fact that most colleges allow students to drop, or withdraw without penalty, from any class as long as they do so by a certain deadline each semester. You don't have to pay for dropped classes, and they are never recorded on your transcript. Use this system to your advantage. At the beginning of every term, sign up for one or two extra courses, and then after the first week drop your least favorite(s).

During that first week, when you are deciding which courses to stick with, make note of the professors' teaching styles, review the syllabi carefully, and skim through the required books at the bookstore. If you are still undecided about whether to drop a specific course, stop by the professor's office hours and have a conversation about the schedule, the workload, and his or her teaching philosophy. See if you can track down other students who have taken this class with this professor. Find out what they think.

This approach might lead to more work for you during the first week of each semester, but remember, one hard week is always better than sixteen. And there is nothing more painful than working like a dog for a class that fails to interest you. Dropping courses every term is like an insurance policy against academic unhappiness. Take advantage of this opportunity.

13

# 4

## Start Long-Term Projects the Day They Are Assigned

14

*College students dread* long-term projects. Why? Because we are really, really bad at them. This is true. At this very moment, at college campuses across the country, students are convincing themselves that just because it's *possible* to complete long-term projects in one frenzied night of panicked work, they *should* follow such a plan. You don't have to be one of these people.

The lure of procrastination is powerful, but you can conquer it by employing one very simple technique: **When assigned a long-term project, finish some amount of work toward its completion that very same day.** This doesn't have to be a major chunk of work. Thirty minutes is enough. Do something simple: jot down a research schedule on your calendar; sketch out an outline; check out and skim the introduction of several relevant books; write a series of potential thesis statements. This is all it takes.

CAL NEWPORT

Once you have accomplished something, no matter how small, you realize that starting your project early is not actually all that bad. In fact, it feels good. You are a step ahead of your entire class, and it was easy to do. This sensation is powerful. Believe it or not, it actually makes you look forward to completing more and more work ahead of schedule, until, before you know it, you'll be finished—and it won't be four forty-three A.M. the morning the project is due.

Of course, this approach is not a miracle cure for completing long-term projects on time. Big college assignments are still really, really hard, and you'll still need to work diligently in order to complete them (see Rule #52, "Keep a Work-Progress Journal," for more help on this subject). However, for whatever psychological reason, doing some work the day a project is assigned seems to have a near-miraculous effect on reducing the tendency to delay. So give this rule a try. There is no reason to let long-term projects force you to scramble like a maniac at the last minute. Start small and start immediately.

# 5

## Make Your Bed

*It turns out* that mom was right; you need to make your bed every morning, preferably immediately after you wake up. Make this an unbreakable habit, like brushing your teeth. But that's not all. You should also never leave clothes lying around your room—put them in a hamper or in your drawers after you change. Put books on the shelves where they belong, and when you are done with papers and notebooks, put them away in your desk. Empty your garbage basket daily.

These are the basic conditions for keeping a clean and organized dorm room, and they are essential. How could something as simple as making your bed have a dramatic impact on your college success? Because a clean room creates a focused mind; a messy room creates a distracted mind. You want a focused mind. The more focused you are, the more effectively you can handle the challenges of being a student. When you are tripping over discarded pizza boxes, sniffing random piles of clothing to find a "clean" pair of socks, and constantly searching under furniture and behind appliances to find that book you need, it's really hard to get energized. Imagine that you have a paper to write. In which instance would it be easier to get started: living in a war zone of a room where your desk is best identified as the boxlike shape under that pile of laundry and discarded Twinkie wrappers, or, alternatively, living in a clean, orderly environment with a clear desk and the resources you need readily at your disposal?

Of course, there is also the possibility of getting stuck with the dreaded messy roommate. In this instance, there is probably not much you can do to change his or her behavior. Trust me, thousands before you have tried. However, this doesn't get you off the hook. Keep your side of the room clean, and take responsibility for the general actions, like emptying wastebaskets, vacuuming, and periodically dusting. This may not sound fair, but it's a small price to pay to win at college.

If you cannot maintain an organized room you will never truly feel that your life is organized. By keeping your living space in order there will be fewer distractions, and you will feel in control of your environment. These traits are absolutely necessary to support ambitious achievement. It hurts, I know. But it is important to keep your room clean. And it will make your mother happy.

# 6

## Apply to Ten Scholarships a Year

18 *One of the* most striking elements of a standout student's résumé is typically the awards and honors section. It's hard not to be impressed when you see scholarship after scholarship piled on top of one another into an inferiority complex–inducing avalanche of accolades. Here is the secret that your neighborhood Rhodes Scholar doesn't want you to know: **Any student can create an impressively large list of awards.** The key is to stop thinking of scholarships and awards as gifts handed down from above to only the most deserving students. The reality is that many scholarships and awards are actually handed down from an overworked, uninterested administrator who was assigned the unfortunate task of choosing a winner from the depressingly small pool of students who actually bothered to apply correctly. Therefore, for a lot of small awards, if you take the time to apply, and demonstrate dili-

**CAL NEWPORT**

gent effort in your application, your odds of winning are quite good. Take advantage of this situation!

Here is what you should do: Contact your dean's office, Career Services Center, and departments relating to your field of study. Ask them for information on scholarships, fellowships, and awards. Also, use Web-based services such as FastWeb (www.fastweb.com) and FinAid! (www.finaid.org) to search for additional national scholarships for which you are eligible. Talk to the companies where your parents, aunts, uncles, and siblings work; find out if they offer any student scholarships. And finally, look for scholarships from companies or organizations in any industry of interest to you. From this large hit list, choose up to ten scholarships that best fit your abilities, passions, and accomplishments. Mark the deadlines on your calendar and apply to every single one of them when the time is right. Do this every year.

While this aggressive approach may force you to sacrifice some hours, by the time you graduate you will have amassed a head-turning list of honors. Think about it. For every ten well-selected scholarships and awards you apply for, you probably have a good shot at winning at least one, and maybe even two or three. And of course, the more scholarships you win, the better your odds on future applications. This means that after four years you can approach the job market (or grad school admissions committees) with quite a few honors listed on your résumé. This is unusual, this is impressive, and it is a great way to gain access to elite opportunities.

# 7

## Build Study Systems

*How do smart* students study? In every bizarre way imaginable. There is the math major who assigns point values to all of his review strategies, and then keeps a spreadsheet to make sure that he covers a certain number of points by exam day. Or there is the French student who creates elaborate quiz show–style games to learn new vocabulary. Or the political science major who creates giant knowledge maps on her wall, linking concepts visually with bright yarn. Smart students build complex study systems. The details of these approaches don't matter, as long as they are specific, regimented, and creative. Follow this example. **You should never begin studying without a systemized plan for what you are going to review, in what format, and how many times.**

Building very specific study systems breaks a formidable task into accomplishable chunks, and it frees up your energy to focus on learning rather than worrying about your state of preparation. Without a study system, you end up wandering haphazardly through the material, staring at a tall stack of books with woe in your heart and resignation on your mind. With a study system, your task becomes tolerable.

Before you even crack your first book, take ten minutes to actually write down exactly how you plan to study. Look at Rules #26 and 70 for some guidance on review techniques that work well. Then build a checklist with big boxes ready to be checked off as the corresponding tasks are completed. Once you are convinced that this study system will adequately prepare you, you can then free yourself from any worries as to whether you will be ready for the upcoming exam. Your responsibilities have been reduced to simply finding the time to plow through every item in your plan.

In addition, the more unusual or creative your system, the better. This will reduce tedium, inject some novelty into the process, and lead to the establishment of stronger mental connections. This is why the aforementioned math major used a point system, the French major designed a quiz show, and the political science major taped yarn to her wall. Their study systems are comprehensive *and* interesting. They are studying smart, and because of this they will do well.

When it comes to studying, the planning is as important as the process. Without a study system, you can end up wasting your time, energy, and potential grade.

# 8

## Befriend a Professor

*Contrary to popular* student belief, professors are not evil lords of academia who swoop down from their ivory towers only to torment you with papers, convoluted syllabi, and blue-book exams. In reality, they are usually quite nice. Even more important, they are a most crucial ally in your quest to maximize your college experience. **If you want to become a standout student, you must befriend a professor.** Make him or her a mentor, someone who is aware of your overall academic plan, your life goals, your concerns, and your triumphs.

A close relationship with a professor will help motivate you to achieve ambitious academic goals and will expose you to exciting new possibilities. Professors are the gatekeepers to student success. They provide the letters of recommendation, informal introductions, and experienced advice that are necessary to win major scholarships, get accepted into competitive programs, land dream internships, be nominated for awards, and, in general, enable you to take advantage of all the opportunities typically offered only to top students. In short, professors provide the fuel for the academic success machine.

Don't worry. Making an ally of a professor is not a difficult task. Professors enjoy interacting with their students; it is often the only feedback they get on how well they are doing their job. To create a meaningful connection, you should begin with regular attendance at office hours. Some students worry that they don't have any specific problems to discuss. The secret is to be observant. There are many more opportunities to speak with a professor than you might realize at first. When you are working on a paper, you can see the professor to talk about possible topics, then again to get feedback on the idea you selected, and then again to check the structure of your argument once you begin writing. When an exam is approaching, you can ask for clarification on particularly difficult material covered in class. And if you are in a technical class, the door is always open to discuss homework problems or concepts that you can't quite grasp.

If these efforts result in a strong rapport, allow your conversations to shift gradually from specific class-related issues to academic advice in general. Keep this dialogue open even after the semester ends, making sure to keep in touch with the professor on a regular basis. Swing by his or her office every once in a while to give an update on how things are going. If the professor offers

23

other courses relevant to your interests, make a point of taking them. By demonstrating such a concentrated effort to learn from the wisdom of your target professor, over time, he or she will develop a vested interest in your success.

This approach is not feckless brown-nosing, so ignore those who suggest otherwise. Befriending a professor is about fulfilling the perfectly natural desire to have a more experienced person guide you through a complicated and exciting period of your life. It's a mutually beneficial relationship that provides the professor with a sense of impact and fulfillment, and provides you with a variety of wonderful new opportunities and counsel. Leave the shiny red apple at home—a serious professorial relationship is a sign of a serious commitment to your academic career.

# 9

**Become a Club President**

*To put it* bluntly, losing students don't think they have enough time to be involved with extracurricular organizations. Average students join extracurricular organizations. And winning students *run* extracurricular organizations. You heard it here first: **You absolutely have the ability to run a campus organization.** This is not something to be afraid of. It's not nearly as complicated or completely time-consuming as you might imagine, and it's definitely within your grasp. In general, if you are a well-organized person, club leadership may be challenging, but it's far from overwhelming. Keep this in mind, because most students sell themselves short and are happy just to be involved. You, however, want to be in charge!

Find a club on campus that excites you and join as soon as possible. Work hard, attend all the meetings, take positions of responsibility whenever they are available, and follow a path into a leadership position.

If you have a strong idea for an organization that doesn't already exist, this is even better. Spend one year working with an existing club to gain an understanding of how student organizations operate at your college. Then petition your school for the resources necessary to start your own.

Why is this a good idea? Because few collegiate experiences are more rewarding than the challenge of running a campus club. You will gain substantial amounts of confidence from leading your fellow students toward a common goal, and you'll maintain a healthy sense of perspective by finding sources of accomplishment unrelated to academic performance. You'll meet people who share your common interests and bond over your shared goals in a way you rarely do in an academic classroom. And of course, when applying for jobs, awards, or competitive programs, being a club president helps you rise above other applicants.

An academic curriculum alone is not enough to keep life at college interesting. But don't waste your free time with scattered, loose commitments; instead, focus on a few concentrated goals. If you are truly interested in becoming a standout, taking control of a campus organization is an excellent start.

## Read a Newspaper Every Day

*If your brain* is a muscle, then reading a newspaper is like mental cal-
isthenics. In order to succeed in an academic environment your mind
has to be constantly energized, confident, and ready to engage. With
this in mind, **you should read a newspaper every day.**

Reading a major newspaper at the same time every day is a
perfect way to juice up your mental energy and prepare you to take
on intellectual challenges. Make it a habit. If they're available, alter-
nate between the *New York Times* and the *Wall Street Journal.* They
are both excellent, and when combined will give you a balanced
world view. If you don't have access to either of these papers, try
*USA Today.* Though perhaps not as in-depth, the reporting is timely,
and it can be fully read in one sitting. As a last resort, you can access most of these newspapers online. The local paper might be interesting, but it's no substitute.

Read every article on the front page, and then read two or three articles of interest from each of the interior sections. Don't just skip right to the sports page. Try to expand your intellectual horizons every day. This regular reading of a major newspaper will keep you current on the state of international and domestic affairs, politics, business, and the fine arts. This in turn will boost your mental energy and confidence, and open you to new perspectives and information that will help your coursework. Reading a daily paper provides essential food for your ambitious brain. Make sure you don't go hungry.

## 11

## Do One Thing Better Than Anyone Else You Know

*If you want* to succeed at college, you have to develop a healthy sense of self-confidence. This doesn't mean you should be arrogant—such people are often secretly insecure. Instead, you want to be self-assured, proud, and modest all at the same time. These are the traits of a well-liked, successful student.

Easier said than done? Not really. One good technique for bolstering your confidence is mastering a skill. Everyone is good at something. All you need to do is to find out what this something is for you, and then practice until you are better at it than any of your friends at school. Be it playing the guitar, writing fiction, shooting hoops, or cooking, **develop a skill you can be known for.** Again, this is not about bragging rights. People can know you are good at something without you having to constantly remind them. This is about reinforcing your identity and sense of self-confidence.

Why is this so important? Because college is an overwhelming social environment. You are thrown into a small space with thousands of other students who know nothing about you. Many students fail to maintain a strong sense of identity in this situation, and instead begin to peg their self-worth on receiving the respect and admiration of others. If you're invited to a hot party, do well on a test, or catch the eye of that cute girl (or boy) ahead of you in the lunch line, you feel good about yourself. But if you end up with no plans for Friday night, bomb a test, or realize that the cute girl was actually smiling at her bodybuilder boyfriend standing right behind you, well, then you feel pretty lousy. The state of your self-esteem is like a roller-coaster ride, differing from day to day depending on events beyond your control. You cannot win at college with this mind-set.

When you are dependent on good things happening to make you feel good, your life becomes centered on preserving a good mood. This will constrain you, because if you are constantly worried about avoiding anything negative, you will never do anything out of the ordinary. Standout students, on the other hand, do very little that *is* ordinary. This is what makes them so phenomenal. They find better ways, uncover new approaches, and question everything. The only way to develop such an aggressive mind-set is to have a strong sense of self-confidence to back you up.

Developing these traits is not easy. But doing one thing better than anyone else you know is an excellent start toward accomplishing this goal. By mastering one activity in your life, you are putting a stake into the ground, giving yourself one thing to feel sure of, and making a declaration about who you are. Don't let others dictate how you should feel about yourself; strengthen your identity—then go conquer your world.

## 12

**Avoid Daily To-Do Lists**

*Time blocking works best.*

32     *For whatever reason,* it's ingrained in students at an early age that the best way to stay organized is to have a daily to-do list. You have probably tried this approach. The idea is to make a list of all the tasks you need to get done, and then cross off the items on the list as you move through your day in an orderly and, above all, predictable manner. Yeah, right!

    Here is the most important rule you will ever hear about student time management: **Daily to-do lists do not work at college.** Your schedule is too complicated and too unpredictable. Some assignments could easily take up your entire evening, while others may take just minutes. Friends will drop by unexpectedly, meals will last for hours, and interesting opportunities for fun will pop up at the last moment. A to-do list can't tame this hectic lifestyle. If you blindly move through the day, trying to accomplish tasks from a list whenever it seems like you have some free time, you will get very little done. Here is a better way to take control of your schedule:

Every morning, before your first class, rip a sheet of paper out of your notebook. Go down the left-hand margin marking the waking hours of the day using every other line as a guide. Now block out the hours you will be in class. Then block out the hours you will be eating meals, and when you will be in meetings or other scheduled events. The white space that remains represents the free time that you have available to work with for the day. This is a great way to visualize your schedule. Now, start partitioning this free time into one-hour increments, and assign these blocks to specific projects and assignments. Set aside at least one block for accomplishing small chores or errands. Next to this space write a small to-do list of the little tasks you need to get done that day. This ensures that even when you have huge projects to work on, the little tasks that keep your world running—buying toothpaste or returning library books—will not be neglected.

Keep this sheet with you and reference it throughout the day to guide your work habits. If you get knocked off schedule, which will happen frequently, simply take out your sheet at the next available calm moment and spend half a minute reorganizing your time for the remaining hours of the day.

This approach only takes two paragraphs to explain, and just minutes a day to implement, but it is exponentially more effective than daily to-do lists. Unless you're a big fan of stress, do yourself a favor and give time-blocking a try. It's a much smarter way to manage your day.

## 13

## Learn to Give Up

*Unless you are* starting in a *Rocky* movie, remember: **Giving up is**
**a tactical skill, not a weakness.** When you are faced with a
project or commitment that threatens to swallow up your entire
life, give up. That's right, give up. Of course, this probably sounds
a little unusual (read: insane) to the many talented students out
there who strongly believe in the power of determination and
willpower. But although steadfast diligence is definitely an ad-
mirable trait, it's worthless at college.

In the intense environment of higher education it's not
enough to just grind away at your problems until they are solved.
You have to be smart about how you parcel out your precious time.
When faced with a difficult problem or demanding commitment,
try to handle it in a reasonable manner—keeping in mind that important tasks often require important amounts of time. However, if

a problem seems unsolvable no matter how hard you try, or a commitment begins taking up a destructively large amount of your schedule no matter how much you delegate, give up.

This doesn't mean you should walk away without a second thought. Instead, make an appointment with your professor or a classmate to help you solve your unsolvable problem. Or, over a reasonable period of time, reduce your involvement with your demanding commitment to free up your schedule appropriately.

Let's look at a few sample scenarios to clarify when you should and should not give up. For example, let's say you are working on an economics problem set, and you have approached the problems with plenty of time and attention but you still can't get the answers. First, make arrangements to get outside help from a professor or T.A. Then move on to something else. Ignore your initial instinct to stay up all night, battling the problems until you collapse from exhaustion.

On the other hand, let's say that you have a new club commitment that requires you to spend a few hours every Tuesday night organizing a campuswide meeting. And let's say that this upsets you because it really reduces the amount of other work you can get done on Tuesdays. This is not a good excuse to give up. You can compensate for the number of work hours you lose on Tuesday by adjusting your Sunday and Monday schedules accordingly. The new commitment is hard, but it's not a waste of energy.

Finally, imagine that your hypothetical club commitment has now expanded greatly, and you find yourself with hours of work to complete almost every day. No matter how carefully you schedule, other parts of your life are being neglected. In this instance, you can't control the time commitment. The sheer weight of tasks has become too expansive for you to complete them in reasonable balance with your other commitments. You need to give up. Delegate a major portion of the work, or step down from your position of power.

In these examples, the key word for deciding whether or not to give up was "productivity." It's okay to spend many hours working on something as long as those hours are productive. In the first example, it's not productive to spend time on problems that you will never fully understand without outside help. Therefore you are smart to give up.

In the second example, the block of time you have to spend on Tuesday nights is productive. You're getting something important accomplished, and you have more than enough advance warning to compensate for the time required. Giving up here would mean missing out on an opportunity whose rewards easily outweigh the cost of rescheduling a couple of work hours once a week.

The third example is a little bit tricky. It may seem like each individual task you do is useful, but it's their sheer cumulative volume that makes your involvement unproductive. If a commitment has no time frame, and it seems like you could push everything else aside and work for days straight without ever fulfilling all that needs to be done, then that commitment is unproductive. The rewards do not outweigh the tremendous time cost. You need to give up or lose your whole schedule to an uncontrollable stream of tasks.

Productive work is any work that is efficiently accomplishable in a known amount of time. If a task has no end in sight, or serious time spent on it accomplishes very little, you need to give up. To learn to give up is to learn to weed out your unproductive commitments so you can maximize what you get done. This is a trait you should develop. Remember, giving up, when done strategically, is not a weakness. It's simply smart life management.

# 14

## Never Nap

*This is very* painful to say, but it's just too important to be ignored. While at college, **do not nap.** (I'll pause to wait for the groaning to die down.) Allow me to explain. Sleeping in the afternoon or early evening takes up large amounts of your limited time, it makes you drowsy and unfocused, and it throws off your regular sleep schedule. Not to mention that this behavior can quickly become an addictive bad habit, where you're regularly losing hours to sleep every afternoon, nights pass fitfully, and staying awake during class becomes a Herculean challenge. Once a napper, always a napper. If due to unavoidable circumstances you find yourself unusually tired during the day, there are other alternatives for rejuvenating your energy that are more effective than napping.

If you are feeling just slightly sluggish in the afternoon, go outside and do some light exercise. A short jog, a game of basketball, a brisk walk—anything that gets your heart pumping will usually pep you right up. If exercising doesn't help, go on the biochemical offensive and target your fatigue with food and drink. Gather up a pile of fresh fruits and a liter of ice-cold water. This is like rocket fuel for your body, and will give you a streak of energy.

If, after all of this, your eyelids are still drooping, don't give in to daytime slumber just yet. Instead, deep-six your difficult studying and turn your attention to simpler tasks. Draw up a to-do list of all the little chores you have been putting off. Vacuum your room. Mail letters. Go to the grocery store. Type up your lecture notes. Organize your class materials. Check out and return library books. Then, and this is the important part, head to bed early and get a full night's rest. The key is to accomplish goals throughout the day while at the same time not throwing off your sleep schedule. One late night should not kill two full days of productivity. By keeping your energy high, and then falling immediately back into a normal sleep routine, you can alleviate the potential nap-induced damage of drowsy days.

40

just by huddling up there. ... actual sentences at least ...

# 15

## Sign Up for Something Your First Week

*The first week* of college is an awkward time to say the least. You don't really know anyone, the proper procedures for using the dining hall remain elusive, and you fear that if one more person tries to make you play a fun get-acquainted icebreaker game you might snap and stab them to death with their own name tag–marker. One reaction to this situation is to become a Freshman Fall Hermit and retreat into the comfort of dorm-room television and studying for classes. This approach is not necessarily as bleak as it may at first sound. Through random encounters you will still begin to meet people despite your best efforts. But the hermit approach denies you a lot of opportunities to get excited early on in your collegiate career. And, of course, excitement and inspiration about your pursuits are the fuel of a successful college student.

So instead of hunkering down and letting your Freshman Fall

pass by harmlessly, embrace it wholeheartedly by signing up for something your first week. It could be an intramural sports team, a publication, an affinity group, the campus radio station, a musical ensemble, or a club that gathers regularly to discuss world issues. There are a staggering number of activities you can potentially join; choose just one that excites you. Your first week is the best time to get involved. You will be one of many new members learning the ropes, you will instantly meet new people, and throughout your first term you will already have a sense of extracurricular purpose. The awkwardness of Freshman Fall disappears when you have a prefab group of acquaintances to say "hi" to as you pass them in the library. And having projects to work on outside of class is a great way to start revving up the ambition and inspiration that will help you win at college.

The happiest students are also the most involved students. When it comes to crafting your slate of collegiate pursuits, the sooner you get involved, the better.

## 16

**Always Be Working on a "Grand Project"**

*Successful, interesting college* students are definitely a varied bunch.    **43**
Yet there is one thing many of them have in common: a wonderful sense of possibility. Whereas most students are content to stay the course, winning students love to get excited about big goals. They crave the thrill of pursuing opportunities that very few people have attempted before them. An average student does well in a science course; a winning student gets involved in original research. An average student sends a letter to the school newspaper; a winning student writes a regular column. An average student wants to join a club; a winning student starts a national organization. **If you want to stand out at college you should foster an attitude of "anything is possible."** And one of the best ways to develop this attitude is to constantly be working on a "Grand Project."

To begin with, reflect on your most heartfelt aspirations. If you could be doing anything five years from now, what would it be? Then design and follow an ambitious Grand Project that moves you toward your answer. For example, if you get excited about the idea of writing for *The New Yorker,* you might create a Grand Project to first publish a series of intelligent nonfiction pieces for your school paper, then a local paper, then a second-tier national publication on your way to the big time. If you dream of screenwriting in Hollywood, you might research a list of every upcoming student-film-writing contest, tack the deadlines on your wall, and work on finishing an original screenplay in time to be submitted to all of them. Or, if you are motivated by young entrepreneur success stories, you might jot down a clever business idea, create a Web site, and launch your very own dorm-room corporation.

Your Grand Project should consist of a group of achievable, nonacademic accomplishments that, when combined, move you closer to an exciting aspiration. Think big. Be ambitious. When you explain a Grand Project to someone it should elicit a response of "Wow!" Working on such a project will keep you constantly excited and energetic. It will keep the pressures of course work in perspective, and make it easy to brush aside the little bad occurrences that pop up now and then. When you work on a highly ambitious project, you feel invincible, like you are a step ahead of the rest of the world, forging unique paths to great success. It doesn't matter if you don't always succeed. The novelty and thrill of taking chances is a powerful force.

This may sound like a bunch of psychobabble, but if you actually try pursuing a Grand Project, you will understand. When you finish that screenplay, see your article in print, or receive your first check as an entrepreneur, the sensation is indescribable. You just accomplished something exciting, and you did so for no other reason than you just wanted to see if it was possible. Once you accomplish one Grand Project, anything seems achievable. This sense of possibility will fuel your rise to becoming a standout.

# 17

**Take Art History and Astronomy**

*Do you know* the difference between the artists Monet and Manet? Can you explain what the cosmological constant is? If you answered "no" to these two questions—or if you answered "yes" but were really just lying to impress someone reading over your shoulder—do yourself a favor and **take art history and astronomy before you graduate.** Of all the courses you could possibly take outside of your major, these two are among the most important.

In the case of art history, take an introductory course that covers the Modern period. In addition to learning the difference between Manet and Monet, study Picasso's formalist innovations and become familiar with the pioneers of the Conceptual Art movement. Contrary to popular belief, art history is surprisingly difficult to learn on your own, and taking a course at college may be your last chance to become culturally literate in the fine arts. This is a skill that will serve you for a lifetime of museum visits and informed cocktail party conversation. More important, learning the central theories behind modern art will give you an overview of the general development of intellectualism in the twentieth century. This may sound snooty, but it's actually quite interesting, and it's an important topic for any student to learn. Understanding the basic tenets of modern and postmodern thinking will provide you with the intellectual ammo you need to tackle the entire medium of the modern fine arts—from paintings, to novels, to plays. And it will also give you a point of reference for understanding modern philosophy and the radical movements of the last century. This is an easy way to make sense of the world of contemporary thought and expression. Don't miss the opportunity!

47

For astronomy, take an introductory course that covers cosmology and the universe. Current understanding of the origins of matter, the expanding cosmos, and the shape of space-time are perhaps some of the most exciting scientific discoveries of all time. Fortunately, when taught in the style of an intro course, these theories are surprisingly easy to understand and unavoidably awe-inspiring. In addition to learning about the history of our world, you will painlessly gain an easy familiarity with the scientific method, which will serve you well in an increasingly technology-oriented age.

In addition to what specifics you learn in these courses, you will benefit by taking a risk and moving beyond your comfort zone when choosing classes. This will fuel your intellectual curiosity and general excitement for knowledge. When you find that you can tackle both Clement Greenberg (the great modern art critic) and Stephen Hawking (the pioneering particle physicist) in the same day, other fields of study will seem more approachable. This kind of curiosity is crucial for happiness and success in any academic environment. Take art history and astronomy, and take them early. Your collegiate experience will be greatly improved.

# 18

## Blow the Curve Once a Term

*Imagine the following* scene: Your professor is handing back a major research paper to your class. The groans that begin to fill the room indicate that the professor was particularly demanding for this assignment. And rightly so, it's worth forty percent of your grade. As he gets to your name, he asks you to stay after class. Uh oh. Nervously you wait as your classmates file out, and when you are the only student remaining in the lecture hall, he walks up to you . . . and then shakes your hand. "Congratulations," he exclaims, "your project was by far the best in the class!"

Sound good? Well, get used to it. If you want to succeed at college, try to put yourself in this situation, in one class, for one assignment, every semester. The advantages of blowing the curve on an assignment are obvious. It will help your grade, the professor will remember and support you with great recommendations and ad-

49

vice, and it will just plain make you feel good about yourself. What is not so obvious is how easy it can be to blow the curve on a regular basis. The key is to pick your spots. To do an outstanding job on every assignment in every class you take would be near impossible. Most assignments are not easily dominated. And to turn heads in a class that is giving you particular trouble, or does not interest you, is difficult. However, it's not so hard to do an outstanding job in a class that you really enjoy, on a project that excites you, assigned during a time where you don't have many competing obligations.

With this in mind, every semester you should choose one class that you like, and within that class choose one interesting project, and then knock it out of the ballpark. Get started very early, work diligently, go above and beyond the stated specifications, and add on extra work to show true intellectual curiosity. If you are writing an art history paper, don't just describe a work as the assignment specifies. Instead, compare it with another work and use it as support for the existence of an abstract theoretical structure you read about in a nonassigned book. If you are working on a computer science programming assignment, schedule yourself to finish a week early so you can add a host of extra bells and whistles. If you have a big economics exam coming up, double the amount of time you normally study and aim for a near-perfect score.

To focus on just one project each term is not all that demanding on your time or energy, especially if you plan ahead and choose an appropriate target. The rewards for this effort can be tremendous.

# 19

**Ask One Question at Every Lecture**

*Keeping alert throughout* a long lecture is not always easy to do. Especially if the class is early in the morning, or held right after a hearty lunch, and it begins to take all of your effort to stop your eyes from drooping . . . drooping . . . ever closer to being . . . closed . . . SNAP! And just like that, the lecture has slipped by without you learning anything other than how to clean drool off your notebook. If you want to succeed at college, you have to do whatever you can to prevent this from happening to you. Fortunately, one of the most effective ways to stay engaged and interested during a lecture is also very easy to do: **Make sure that you always ask at least one question at every lecture.**

The night before, when you are doing the reading that will be covered in the lecture, jot down a quick list of questions that seem relevant. Then, once in class, follow the professor's material

51

carefully, modifying and honing your questions as appropriate. Finally, when you feel you have a question that is meaningful, and will clarify an important point of the discussion, ask away. The key is to stay involved while, at the same time, not acting like the obnoxious kid in the front row who asks random questions every thirty seconds or so.

This approach not only helps you clarify the material and reinforce your understanding, it also keeps your attention focused and ensures that you stay alert. It's a powerful technique for resisting the urge to drift off into a boredom-infused stupor. One or two good questions a class is enough to keep the professor happy, but not enough to solicit the annoyance of your classmates.

52    Take the time to ask at least one question at every lecture. It's simple, and it will redefine your classroom experience for the better.

## 20

**Jump into Research as Soon as Possible**

*Don't take this* the wrong way, but college professors have a life out- 53
side of you and your classes. While most professors enjoy teaching
undergraduates, their professional obligations go far beyond the
classroom. The primary responsibility of a professor at any university
or research institution is the vaguely defined goal of "advancing
knowledge" in their field. And the bulk of this knowledge advance-
ment takes place in the form of original research and academic publication. To put it simply: **Research is where all the action is.** If
you really want to stand out at your college, you need to be in the
middle of this action. You need to be involved with the machinery of
original research that is going on all around you. You need to tap
into the incredible opportunities offered to you, the undergraduate,
to actually make a difference in the world of academia.

Why? First of all, working on real research is like strength training for your intellect. It's challenging, enlightening, and rewarding all at the same time. Once you have worked on writing a peer-reviewed journal article, your paper for Government 101 will seem trivial. Second, it's impressive. Regardless of what you want to do after college, the fact that you did original research sends all the right messages—you're smart, you're driven, you're a cut above the rest. And third, there is no way to become closer to a professor than to spend a weekend in a biology lab with him or her. If you make yourself indispensable in a research setting, the professor will return the favor in the form of recommendations and support.

Timing is important here. If you get involved too late in your collegiate career, you may not have enough time to make an impact. Spend your freshman year getting a good feel for what fields you are interested in. Toward the end of your last freshman semester, begin to inquire about research opportunities. Simply go to the relevant departmental Web sites and read about ongoing research projects. E-mail those professors whose work interests you. Tell them you are interested in getting more experience in the academic world. Mention some specifics of their particular research projects to impress them, and then ask if they are in need of an undergraduate research assistant. Even if they say no, they will probably be able to point you in the direction of someone who does need help. Also, keep your eyes open for undergraduate research grants that might be available. These make it a lot easier to find someone who is willing to bring you on to their project. It's as simple as that.

A common misconception among students is that research only happens in scientific fields. This is far from true. English professors publish articles in academic journals just as regularly as biology professors. While working with the former might involve tracking down references and copying book chapters, and the latter might focus on setting up lab environments and calculating results, the benefits of working on both types of projects are the same. Regardless of your field, there is always some research with which you can assist.

Another misconception is that research is only conducted at large universities. While it's true that big research institutions focus on research more than smaller liberal arts schools, this doesn't mean that the smaller schools aren't still working on projects. In fact, at a small school you have the advantage that there are fewer undergraduates to help with research, meaning that you will most likely end up with even more interesting opportunities from which to choose.

Getting involved with research early is like drinking an elixir of success. It's one of the most commonly overlooked and effective secrets for winning at college. Don't let this opportunity pass you by.

# 21

## Pay Your Dues

*If getting involved* with original research is one of the best things you can do as an undergraduate, then getting involved and acting as if you are somehow entitled to responsibility is one of the worst. The reason you begin research work early in your college career is so you have time to learn and time to prove yourself. **During your first year assisting on a research project, you have to pay your dues.** Don't expect anything. Just be as helpful as possible. Be available. Get work done on time. Make life easier for your research team.

Once you have a good feel for the project, you can begin to modestly boost your involvement. Try using the phrase: "If you think I can handle this, I would be happy to help." In this way, you can angle for more responsibility without coming across as brash. You will simply sound as if you are trying to be helpful, which you are. When you are given more important work to complete, treat each of these early assignments as if it's your doctoral dissertation. Wow those overseeing your work with your diligence and ability. If you do this, you will be a departmental star by the time you graduate. If you instead act ungrateful, demand responsibility early, and sulk when delegated boring tasks, you will upset professors and develop a negative reputation.

If you pay your dues with grace and enthusiasm and are mindful of the opportunity you are receiving, you will maximize the many positive benefits of participating in original research work.

# 22

## Study in Fifty-Minute Chunks

*According to conventional* wisdom on college campuses, the most effective way to tackle a large amount of studying is to: (1) pile all of your books, notes, and review sheets in front of you; (2) study until you collapse; (3) awaken several hours later wondering where you are; (4) wipe the drool off your books with a damp, warm washcloth; (5) consume large quantities of caffeine; (6) repeat. **Do not do this** (except for the part about the damp, warm washcloth . . . that really is the best way to clean up drool). When you do schoolwork, be it reading, taking notes, working on a lab, or memorizing verbs, try to do everything in fifty-minute chunks. Take ten-minute breaks in between each fifty-minute chunk. This is key for any successful student.

Why fifty minutes? For one thing, there are compelling scientific rationales. Those who study cognition can draw maps of memory retention over time, and demonstrate how periods of roughly fifty minutes, divided by short breaks, will maximize the amount of material you can successfully learn and remember in a given sitting. But just as important, breaking down all your work into distinct, known periods of time provides structure for your studying. If you have five hours of reading to do, that stack of books in front of you can seem hopeless. How can you focus on the first chapter when there are so many to follow? But if you only have to stay focused for fifty minutes at a time, then the impossible suddenly seems possible. Five work chunks doesn't seem so bad. You could do three before dinner and two after, or whatever seems easiest, and suddenly your assignment is approachable. Not to mention that you are learning the material in the most effective way possible for the human brain.

In general, as discussed in Rule #7, Build Study Systems, you never want to approach any large amount of studying or reading or note-taking without some sort of structure. Using fifty-minute chunks is a great addition to any such structure.

# 23

## Schedule Your Free Time

60  *Free time is* both a blessing and a curse for a successful college student. On the one hand, most of your fondest memories will come from hanging around with your friends, talking, playing video games, and watching indecipherable Japanese kids' shows on the Cartoon Network (trust me). On the other hand, it is dangerously easy to lose too much productivity to the allure of recreation. You would be surprised by how simple it can become to convince yourself to take yet another big break, even when you know that you have a lot of work waiting to be completed. You could also find yourself suffering from an even worse problem, which is feeling guilty every time you try to relax, worrying that there is probably some work you could be doing right then. You don't want to deal with either of these afflictions.

Fortunately, there is an unconventional yet simple way to both avoid these problems and ensure that you get the perfect amount of rest and relaxation: **Schedule your free time.** Most people consider free time to be any time when they are not explicitly working. All you need to do is flip this understanding, and say that work time is any time that you are not explicitly relaxing. When you create your schedule each morning, you need to do two things. First, choose an end point for the day. For example, you might say that ten P.M. is the end of your workday, and from that point on you will just relax until you go to sleep. Second, decide exactly when you are going to relax throughout the day. For example, you might decide that you will spend a half hour after lunch watching TV, two hours in the afternoon to go to the gym and hang out with friends, and an hour or two surrounding dinner to unwind. The rest of your time you will be working. As you move through your day, there will never be any question as to whether you should be relaxing. Either you are in one of your scheduled break periods, or you are working. Not only does this cut down on impromptu breaks, but it can also increase your work ethic— everyone works harder right before a scheduled reprieve.

By reversing the way you think about free time, not only will you work more, but when you do relax, you will relax better. There is no fear that you are being irresponsible, or neglecting something important. Scheduling your free time may sound a little scary at first, but it shouldn't. You are not actually reducing—

61

or increasing—the amount of free time you have during the day, you are just labeling and consolidating it so you can maximize the benefits of kicking back. Scheduling your free time is quite simply a win-win proposition, and a great way to painlessly improve your productivity.

## 24

## Dress Nicely for Class

*Track pants, a* slightly stained T-shirt, flip-flops, and a baseball cap
do not count as "getting dressed" in the morning. Nor does it
count if you are wearing any article of clothing that you slept in the
night before, or frequently wear to the gym. You should always
take the time to brush your teeth, shower, tame your hair, and put
on a good-looking outfit every morning before heading to class.
This doesn't mean you must look as if you just jetted in from Mi-
lan, but on the other hand, you shouldn't look like you just got released from a prison chain gang either.

Why bother dressing nicely for class? Two reasons. One, it
makes you feel better about yourself. If you look good, you can
imagine that cute guy or dimpled girl in the front row shooting
some glances in your direction. This will make you happy. And

when you are happy, you have more energy and pay attention better in class. Two, it makes the day official. When you look like you just rolled out of bed, it's all too easy to imagine rolling back in. If you dress nicely, you are sending yourself the message that you are ready to get started and attack the day.

## 25

## Decorate Your Room

*This rule may* apply more to the gentlemen than to the ladies, since, for whatever reason, college-age men tend to have a noted deficiency when it comes to personalizing their living space. Or to put it another way: I have seen WWII–era foxholes with more personality than some guys' dorm rooms. And just to be clear on definitions, the following items don't count as legitimate decoration: any poster involving the movie *Animal House*, Jimi Hendrix, Bob Marley, or Will Ferrell; any photographic portrait originally published in *Maxim*, *Stuff*, or *Sports Illustrated*; any item that may, with a certain probability, have spent a healthy chunk of its previous existence adorning the wall of a bar or liquor store.

**Your room decor should create a space that is both comfortable and a healthy reflection of your personality.** This doesn't necessarily mean going crazy with fancy furniture, walls of quirkily framed photographs, sheets that match a coordinated rug and curtains set, or, God forbid, Christmas lights. But it does mean moving beyond barren walls punctuated only with the occasional predictable poster.

Why decorate? Because it will have a positive effect on your mood and energy. To wake up, go to sleep, and take breaks throughout the day in a personalized and comfortable room is refreshing. Going to classes, studying for tests, and writing papers is stressful, and having a comforting environment to retreat to is a great way to release tension. Not to mention that people like to hang out in comfortable places. A well-designed student pad will attract more visitors, which will also help your mood and social life. If your room is just a starkly lit white cell, you are never going to feel completely relaxed. And this means the tensions that build throughout the day will never completely be released. Over time, this will sap your energy and diminish your performance as a student. Your surroundings really do make a difference.

Find something that truly interests you and incorporate it into your space. Are you a guitar player? Mount your guitars on a wall. Are you a fan of Asian art? Buy three matted black frames, put a print in each, and hang them in an aesthetically pleasing row above your desk. Are you a movie buff? Find posters for two or three movies that you think are particularly influential. Frame them in cheap poster frames of the type you can easily buy at Wal-Mart. Hang them on a wall, and mount a little light above or below each.

While you are at it, find an alternative to the fluorescent

lights in your room. Two good floor lamps and a solid desk lamp can fill your room with a nice incandescent glow. Put a rug on the floor, as cheap carpet or tile is depressing when left uncovered. And buy a piece of furniture that makes you happy. Maybe find a beat-up sofa, or a used armchair, or anything comfortable that you can sink down into while you watch TV or read a book.

There is of course no need to attack your one-room double with a precriminal Martha Stewart–style zeal, but take the time to make your space relaxing. These little touches make a difference.

# 26

## Start Studying Two Weeks in Advance

*For the sake* of argument, let's just say that you need roughly 15 hours to prepare for a big exam. That doesn't sound too bad. If you wake up at nine A.M. the day before, it seems like you would have plenty of time to prepare. Just to be sure, let's do some quick calculations. On a typical day we might use 2 hours for meals, 3 hours for classes, 1½ hours for breaks, 2 hours for the gym, 1½ hours for meetings, and 2½ hours for other homework. Now, with this in mind, if we start studying at nine A.M. the day before, we should be done with our 15 hours by around . . . noon the next day! Hmmm, maybe that doesn't work too well.

If we spread our studying over two days, we can now finish our 15 hours by only having to stay up until five-thirty each of the two mornings. Again, not that great.

If we spread our studying over three days, we will get to sleep by a much more reasonable two-thirty each of those three mornings. Ugh. As you can see, though 15 hours doesn't seem too bad at first, when we start to fit this allotted time into an already busy schedule, we realize just how many days we actually need to prepare for an exam without sacrificing copious amounts of sleep and sanity. Now, think what would happen if we had *two* exams to prepare for? Or a paper to write at the same time? This could get ugly.

The point of this depressing arithmetic is to highlight the reality of preparing for big exams: **You have to start studying well in advance.** Your schedule is busier than you think, and if you leave a large chunk of studying until the last days before an exam, you will be forced to sacrifice.

To avoid unnecessary pain, a good rule of thumb is to begin studying two weeks in advance. Now, before you accuse me of being certifiably insane, let me make this clear: I do not mean that you should start hard core all-day study sessions fourteen days before the exam (this book is about how to win at college, not how to become the world's biggest tool). Instead, I am suggesting that you conduct no hard core all-day study sessions ever again. Break up those fifteen hours of studying into many painless one- or two-hour chunks, and you'll dominate the exam without any headaches. Of course, the only way for this to work is to spread out all those harmless little chunks over a longer period of time. Hence the two weeks.

For the first week, just put in an hour or so of work on most days. Build your study system to allow for many small chunks of work, make the material familiar, and get a good feel for the information. Tack on a couple extra hours of studying over the weekend, and you'll already have ten hours of review under your belt with seven days to spare without having to work more than an hour or two at a time. As you come into the week before the exam, keep studying just an hour or so a day, racking up your review hours and moving through your study system slowly but steadily. And then, during the final two days before the exam, put in longer three-hour sessions to really cement the now very familiar material into your mind. By the time your pen hits paper on the big day you will be untouchable! The exam won't stand a chance. And best of all, you got prepared with no late nights, no all-day study grinds, and no caffeine-induced hallucinations that your art history textbook is trying to poison you.

70

Studying two weeks in advance may sound crazy at first. But once you realize that you are just spreading the necessary work out over time, not increasing the total amount of work you do, you should come to understand that this approach is a painless and highly effective method for test preparation. If you fear that you lack the willpower to get started so early, I challenge you to try this approach just once. Do it for a test early in the term when you don't feel so overwhelmed by other obligations. After you have experienced the joy of dominating a test without any hard work, I guarantee you will be converted.

*Your number-one* most important skill as a college student is writing
ability. Your second most important skill as a college student is writing ability. Your third most important skill as a college student is,
you guessed it, writing ability. And so on.

You probably get the point here: **Writing is really, really
important for a college student.** You will succeed academically only if you have the ability to express your thoughts clearly
and convincingly. This means that if you want to win at college,
you need to be good at writing. *Really* good at writing.

A good analogy is that writing is to a college student what
shooting hoops is to a basketball player. If you want to be a standout basketball player, you stick around after practice and shoot extra baskets. If you want to be a standout college student, you have
to stick around after you are done with your assignments and do

some extra writing. You can accomplish this by joining the staff of a publication on campus. It could be the daily newspaper, a writing magazine, a science journal, a political paper, or a humor rag. It doesn't matter what publication you choose as long as it requires you to write well and write often. You can also write guest opinion pieces, offer to tackle proposal writing for clubs you are involved with, or send well-crafted letters to local politicians and newspapers. If you are creative, you can write short stories, tackle screenplays, or craft reviews for the arts section of a student paper. The specific format isn't important, just as long as you are writing. The more words you transfer from your head to paper, the better you will become at this vital craft.

Adopt the mind-set of Larry Bird. It didn't matter if he was happy or sad, energized or tired, every day he would shoot hundreds of baskets. You should do the same. Force yourself to write as much as possible. It is an essential, irreplaceable skill for succeeding at college. Master it.

# 28

## Eat Alone Twice a Day

*At college, meals* tend to be like an organizational black hole—they unexpectedly suck hours of free time out of your day. By the time you gather a group of friends, find a table at a dining hall, eat a meal, shoot the breeze, finally break away from the group, and re-build your focus enough to get back to work, your simple meal has transformed into a major time commitment. Don't get the wrong idea, **taking the time to eat a social meal with your friends is a great idea; just don't do it more than once a day.**

Eat breakfast in your dorm room, or grab a quick bite on the way to your first class. Mornings are painful, so you are not miss-ing much in terms of company. If you have a busy night ahead of you, arrange to eat lunch with your friends. Then, later, you can get your dinner to go and eat it in your dorm room, barely interrupt-ing your work cycle. If you're facing a busy afternoon and an easy night, then arrange to meet your friends for dinner. Eat a quick lunch alone in the dining hall over a newspaper between tasks on your daily schedule.

Frequent, long meals are a schedule spoiler for successful students. This rule is simple, but it will keep you both efficient and social.

*College may be* the best four years of your life. But it will probably be some of the most intense as well. Think about it. You are thrown into a close-knit world where you have no personal space, you are living with strangers, your mind is being challenged more than ever before, you have to form an entire social identity from scratch, and for the first time there is no one providing you with any direct guidance on how to live your life. And that's just the first week! Throw in the stresses of exam periods, student competition, and relationships, and some would say that the pressures of going to college become a lot like the pressures of going to war—that is, if wars were sponsored by J. Crew. But don't panic. The key to surviving this emotional roller coaster is savoring the highs (of which there are many) and avoiding the lows (which, since you're reading this book, will hopefully be few and far between). And one successful technique for keeping yourself balanced and happy during the tough times at college is to find an escape.

Preferably, your escape should be a place or activity that is far removed from your typical life as a college student. **You need to journey to a place where you will be cut off from everyday student life,** a place that provides you with a chance to relax and regain your sense of identity. The Student Union doesn't count. Your dorm TV lounge doesn't count. Your friend's room down the hall certainly doesn't count. To misquote a once famous line: You need to get the hell out of Dodge. Going to Barnes & Noble, grabbing a stack of books, and reading them over a cup of gourmet coffee is a good example of a great escape. So is taking a long drive in the country, or going for a long jog at an off-campus park. Schedule an escape for yourself every single week. And do it alone. Treat it like taking medicine.

College only becomes overwhelming when you let it consume your entire life. If you make a point to regularly escape from the world of roommates, tests, late papers, and parties, your collegiate stresses can be kept in check. Escape well, and escape often; you'll be surprised at how easy it can be to navigate the emotional ups and downs of college life.

# 30

## Take Hard Courses Early On

*Here is a* simple rule for choosing courses early on in your collegiate

career: **No more than half of your scheduled courses should include the word *intro* in the title** (and absolutely none should include the phrase *for fun and profit*). Introductory courses are a great way to become broadly familiar with an unfamiliar subject. This is especially true for fields like art history or political science, where there is a basic body of knowledge you need to recognize before studying any one topic in more detail. However, the problem with intro courses is that they often bear very little resemblance to what other courses in that major will actually be like.

If you are interested in potentially majoring in a particular subject, you need to start taking higher-level courses as soon as possible. This is the only way to get the exposure necessary to make the right decisions about your studies. It also reduces your future course burden as you try to fulfill all the major requirements. And, in general, taking hard courses early on will help speed up your development of crucial collegiate skills—a terrific advantage for any ambitious student.

Don't worry about higher-level courses being too difficult for you. The key is to seek out classes that will be challenging but don't require you to possess a vast amount of prior knowledge. Pay careful attention to any specified requirements. If there are no requirements, or only "recommended" requirements, then you should be okay taking the course even as a freshman. If you're still in doubt about the relative difficulty, e-mail the professor. Briefly explain your background, that you are very interested in the subject matter, and that you would like to get his or her opinion as to whether the workload will be manageable.

Intro courses are useful in moderation, but in abundance they can stunt your growth as a student and leave you feeling bored and uninspired by an otherwise interesting subject. Take that upper-level course! The sooner you immerse yourself in serious collegiate study the more you will get out of your experience. As one successful student put it: "Why waste your time and money in the minor leagues of college courses when you have the ability to be swinging in the majors."

## 31

## Don't Study in Your Room

*If there was* an official ranking of the absolute worst places to study, your dorm room would probably fall somewhere between the New Jersey Turnpike and a Metallica concert. Studying in your dorm room has only one advantage going for it: convenience. Unfortunately, this doesn't count for much, as studying is not supposed to be convenient, it's supposed to be effective. And the most effective place to study is an environment that inspires you to think intelligently, an environment without any unnecessary distractions or temptations for distraction. Or, to put it more plainly, **STUDY AT THE LIBRARY!**

In the Ten Commandments for getting good grades, *Thou shall not study in thy room* is commandment one through five; it's that important. Take a moment to reflect on your dorm room: it's crowded; people are coming and going; every possible distraction from TV to food to video games to AOL Instant Messenger are within easy reach; the building is noisy; you are surrounded by friends. If you want to be productive you have to escape from this environment.

Set aside a large block of time every day to spend studying at the library. Make it the place where you accomplish your most demanding schoolwork. Because it's inconvenient to walk to the library and settle into a study spot, you will be less likely to leave on a whim. Because the library environment is quiet without many distractions, you will have an easier time concentrating, and thus get more quality work done faster. And because the library surrounds you with row after row of solemn academic tomes and diligently studying students, it will be easier for you to get into that high-powered, intellectual zone.

Libraries were designed to maximize your academic productivity. Dorm rooms seem to be designed to minimize it. Successful students recognize that it's not enough to just get through your schoolwork, you also have to give yourself every opportunity to do the work effectively. And besides, the more efficiently you complete your assignments, the more guilt-free time you can spend adding to the entertaining chaos that is your dorm life. When it comes time to study, go where it counts.

## 32

## Don't Study in Groups

*As long as* we are trying to take all the fun out of studying, here is

another stab to the heart: **Don't study in groups.** At first glance,
multiperson study sessions seem to have a lot of advantages: they
are social; they hold you accountable for learning material; they reduce the amount of material you have to study on your own; and
they provide a safety net of people to help you understand difficult
topics. Unfortunately, study groups also tend to have a rather major strike against them. They don't work!

The best way to learn difficult material is to go over it by
yourself, with a lot of concentration, again and again and again until the concepts become second nature. There is no substitute for
this type of learning. As boring or daunting as it may seem, you
really do need to sit at your quiet desk in the library and absorb the
material in all its detail. A member of a study group breezily ex-

plaining the topics to you is not the same thing. In fact, "learning" a concept from a group member is the study equivalent of trying to speed-read a book. You might get the gist of it, but you won't remember or understand the specifics. Spending time with the material by yourself, until you fully understand it, will always be more effective than having someone else paraphrase it for you. And when it comes to efficiency, let's not even get started on the obscene amount of study-group time that is inevitably sacrificed to the gods of gossip.

This doesn't mean that you must be completely isolated when you study. On the contrary, when you want to test your understanding of a concept, or are having trouble with a particular

problem, interacting with other people is very helpful. The key, however, is to seek out someone for specific help on a specific issue, then return to your solo work. Instead of organizing a study group, arrange for some classmates to study at the library at the same time as you, so they will be available to provide focused help as issues arise.

This is how top students tame difficult material. Leave group studying to elementary school kids and law students—the truth is that undergraduates learn best through a little lonely concentration.

## 33

### Join an Honors Program

*This rule is* a little complicated because the definition of an "honors program" differs from school to school. At some colleges you are accepted into an honors program before you ever set foot on campus, and you spend your entire collegiate career living with and taking courses only with honors students. At other colleges the program describes a track of special courses you take in addition to your normal courses. And at still other colleges it's just a title bestowed upon you if you get good grades and attend some special seminars your senior year. **Regardless of the specifics at your school, if there is any possible opportunity to join an honors program, go for it!** These programs generally represent a slightly better version of your college. The classes are smaller, the professors more interested, the students more inspiring. To put it bluntly, an honors program will provide you with a better education

83

than a regular academic program. You will be challenged more, you will learn more, and you will fulfill more of your potential as a student. In addition, having an honors designation on your diploma will go a long way when looking for postgraduation opportunities.

Why would anyone not take advantage of this opportunity? The biggest flaw of honors programs is that they tend to scare students away. "I don't think I'm smart enough" is a typical excuse for not joining an advanced program. This is nonsense. Sure, the classes may require a little more work, but they also provide a better classroom environment, more attention from the professor, and smarter peers, so the extra work is not necessarily harder to complete. And even if you do have to study a little bit more than some of your friends, who cares!?

As long as you are paying so much money to attend college, you might as well maximize what you get out of your investment. If you can get into an honors program, do so. No excuses.

# 34

## Do Schoolwork Every Day

*Being a college* student is a lot like being a professional golfer. As anyone who follows the game will tell you, golf is all about streaks. Regardless of how good a player is, he or she will still have good streaks and bad streaks. If they are in the zone, every shot flies right where they want it. If they fall into a slump, every shot seems to have a personal vendetta against them. College is surprisingly similar. You will go days where your concentration is unbreakable. You will be getting your work done efficiently and effectively. You will be ahead of schedule, on top of your obligations, and feeling good about yourself. Then you will hit a bad streak. Days will pass when you barely crack a book. You will feel tired, bored, and uninspired.

One of the keys to succeeding at college is preventing these slumps from happening. And thankfully, unlike in golf, this goal is actually easy to achieve. The key is consistency. Student slumps occur when you take a long break from work and then find yourself unable to easily pull yourself back into a working rhythm. In order to deny the opportunity for this to occur, **you should do some amount of schoolwork every single day.** This doesn't mean giving up your weekend social plans and becoming an interminable grind. It doesn't matter how much schoolwork you complete; just as long as you do something every day you will have a much easier time staying in the zone. Do an hour of work right after classes on Friday so you have something to feel good about. Don't stay in on Saturday night, but do try to knock off an assignment or two in the afternoon when everyone else is still only semiconscious. Sunday is a workday, you'll just have to get over it. And there are few good reasons for taking a weekday off.

When you complete schoolwork, you feel motivated. When you complete schoolwork every single day, you will feel motivated every single day. By denying yourself long breaks from studying, you deny yourself the chance to fall into a nonworking slump from which it can be hard to escape. A consistent daily commitment to schoolwork will create a powerful cycle of reinforcement and productivity, a cycle which will ensure that you remain the Tiger Woods of academic achievement.

## Attend Guest Lectures

*Colleges attract interesting* visitors. Famous academics, politicians,
policymakers, and authors are always traipsing through campuses
around the country. And most everywhere they stop, they take the
time to give a guest lecture. **You should try to attend at least
two guest lectures every month.** You might think these talks
will be boring, and some of them are (e.g., "The diminishing radii
of poplar saplings in the deciduous forests of Pennsylvania"). But a
lot of guest lectures are not only not boring, they are downright inspiring. If you are an art history major and you take the time to see
a smart, cutting-edge historian speak, you will feel inspired by the
thought of excelling in your field. If you are interested in government and you go to watch a political candidate or policymaker
hold court, you will walk away energized about the possibility of a
future in politics. If you are an aspiring writer, and you hear a suc-

cessful author describe her paths to success, you will be motivated to rush home and fire up your word processor.

This is why you should make a concerted effort to attend guest lectures on a regular basis. You're not doing it to learn more, or to impress your professors (though it does impress them), or to overcome insomnia. You do it to ignite some passion within yourself. You attend to remind yourself of where your hard work is taking you. You attend to get so excited about a topic and your potential that you end up having a hard time falling asleep that night. Getting fired up, once or twice a month about subjects that interest you, will go a long to way to helping you succeed. Go to guest lectures and keep your intellectual fires stoked.

*Exercising has an* almost magical effect on students. The boost in
physical energy and mental motivation that results from a quick,
hard workout is better than any caffeine high. And everyone feels
good about themselves when they come out of the gym feeling
honed and ripped. The problem here, however, is that motivating
a college student to exercise regularly is about as easy as selling a
"I love NY!" T-shirt to a Red Sox fan. Which is to say, it's hard. But
this doesn't mean you should give up.

What's the solution? Stop trying to convince yourself. **Don't
let the decision to exercise become a debatable question.**
Instead, make it a habit, like going to class or brushing your teeth.
On Mondays, Wednesdays, and Fridays always hit the gym. Do it
at the exact same time, for the exact same duration. If you are exercising for energy and health (as opposed to a desire to develop

89

grapefruit-size biceps), you should create a fast routine. Use only a one-hour burst of activity in which to get to the gym, work out, and return to your dorm room. Quick routines are more time efficient and thus easier to schedule consistently. If possible, plan your routine to take place early in the afternoon or morning when you are less likely to be distracted by other commitments. Make this nonnegotiable. If you are using the gym on Mondays, Wednesdays, and Fridays, then set aside time on Tuesdays and Thursdays to do some cardio. On Saturday and Sunday, if you have the time and energy, do a supplementary light workout. However, taking these two days off is excusable; just remember to keep those school-week workouts nonnegotiable.

90      By making your workouts fast, and doing them at the same time every day, you'll end your need to win a mental debate every time you think you should exercise. Conserve your willpower for more important battles, like unplugging your cable when the Food Network's all-day *Iron Chef* marathon comes on during reading period. Keep yourself active and you will keep yourself successful.

**Stay in Touch**

*College is exciting.* College is busy. But most of all, college is a demanding mistress that can suck you wholeheartedly into its isolated womb,
cutting you off from all that once defined your life before you crossed
its ivy-covered threshold. Which is all just an adjective-rich way of saying: **Stay in touch with your friends from back home.**

It can be surprisingly easy to lose touch with the important
people in your life. College is so socially, mentally, and physically
consuming that if you don't make a specific effort to keep in touch,
you will lose your connection to your back-home buds. Why is it
important that you keep these old friendships alive? Because your
old friends know you better than your college friends. When you
go through rough times, a phone call to a friend from home will
pick you back up. You will never feel lonely. Your sense of personal
identity will remain strong. And most important, if you lose contact

with your friends, you will have nothing to do when you go home for the holidays.

To successfully stay in touch with someone means that you must talk with him or her at least once a month. And, this is important, AOL Instant Messenger does not count. Nor does forwarding your friend a link to an unforgivably stupid animation you found on the Internet. You need to actually call on a phone and have voice-to-voice contact.

Talking to four or five of your closest friends, just once a month, is no big deal in terms of time commitment. But the benefit in terms of strengthening your relationships is great. You never realize how important your back-home friendships are until you begin to lose them. Stay in touch.

# 38

## Tack on an Extra Major or Minor

*Tack on an extra major or minor!? Are you kidding me!? I don't have*
*that sort of time! Jerk!* These are common reactions to this uncommon request. Tacking on an extra major or minor is a good thing
for obvious reasons. You will come away from college with in-depth
knowledge of more than one field. It will help you focus during
your undergraduate years. And most important, it looks damn impressive when looking for a job, applying to graduate school, or
winning awards and scholarships. And although many people perceive adding an extra major or minor to be a huge time drain, the
good news is: this is simply not true.

Adding another area of concentration doesn't mean you
have to take any more courses than you normally would. Let's say
that you have one major, and in a typical term you take five
courses: two for your major, and three random elective courses. If

you tacked on another minor, guess what, in a typical term you are still only taking five courses. Except now you are just swapping one of your electives for a minor course. It's no big deal! There is no real difference between a course you choose randomly and a prese- lected course needed for an extra major or minor. They are both college courses, they are worth the same amount of credits, they both interest you, and they both require roughly the same amount of work. **The point here is that tacking on an extra major or minor is not a major hardship.** On the contrary, it's just a way of focusing your decision of what classes to take each term. And focusing is good. It sends the message to yourself, and the world, that you are a serious student with serious interests.

94          The key to painlessly adding a new concentration is to plan well and to plan early. As soon as you decide what your second ma- jor or minor will be, take a night to examine the requirements and course offerings in detail. Lay out a nicely distributed plan of what courses you will take and when. Then just follow this plan each sub- sequent semester when you select your classes. This is all you need to do.

On the other hand, if you are already far along in your aca- demic career, hope is still not lost. Many students come amazingly close to completing the required courses for an extra major or mi- nor without even realizing it. Take a good look at your transcript. Are there any subject areas where you have taken a fair number of classes outside of your primary focus? For most students the answer here is yes. There is the English major who because of a study abroad program has racked up a lot of French credits, or the computer science major who has been taking art history courses off and on for the last couple of years, or the engineering student who gets a thrill out of psychology seminars. For any such secondary cluster of courses on your transcript, look up how many credits away you are from a second major or minor. The results are often surprising. It's quite common for a junior, or fall semester senior, to realize that if he just takes two or three more specific courses, he can tack on a minor he never knew he was pursuing.

If you are going to take the same basic number of classes during your four years of college, no matter what you decide to study, you might as well squeeze as many concentrations as possible out of your experience. As hard as it might be to give up an Underwater Basket Weaving elective, successful students extract as much as possible out of their academic career. So tack on that extra major or minor and maximize your achievements as an undergraduate.

# 39

**Meet Often with Your Adviser**

*Most likely, you* will be assigned an academic adviser your freshman year. This person, usually a professor, is available to provide you with carefully considered advice and to help you construct an academic path properly suited to your abilities and interests. In theory, this sounds like a good idea, but here is how it typically plays out: (1) you meet with your adviser your first week of school, you tell him what classes you signed up for, and he gives his approval; (2) two years pass without any further contact; (3) you encounter your adviser in a hallway, and unsure as to whether you should say "hi," you end up smiling like a shy schoolgirl and manage only an embarrassed, spasmodic nod.

Avoid this awkwardness by making your academic adviser an ally early on. Remember Rule #8, "Befriend a Professor"? All of those benefits of professorial friendship apply here. The key to handling advisers is to give them the opportunity to advise. Come to your first scheduled adviser meeting with a list of questions. Press your adviser for his or her wisdom on choosing majors, handling distributive requirements, finding the best, most worthwhile courses, and learning general strategies for keeping on top of your workload. Feel free to e-mail additional questions as the term goes on. Take the time to set up an appointment at the beginning of each semester to make sure you're on the right track. The secret here is that you, the student, have to take the initiative to make your adviser useful. Treat him or her as a freebie academic ally, given to you by the college. With a little bit of persistence, and much less overall work than it takes to befriend a professor from scratch, you can form a fledgling mentor relationship before your first semester as a freshman is over. This can be an important source of wisdom, inspiration, and advice. If you empower your adviser to help you, a valuable connection will form. This connection is yours to lose or embrace. Don't let a potentially beneficial relationship with your adviser pass you by.

97

# 40

## Don't Get a Normal Job

*For all you* slackers out there, don't start celebrating just yet. Allow me to first clarify this rule. There is nothing wrong with getting a job at college. Many students need the money for work-study and financial-aid packages, and in fact, many students also report that the responsibility of a part-time job puts some much-needed structure into their lives. The key factor here is what type of job you get.

Don't work retail in town. Don't serve food at a local restaurant. Don't paint houses or help move furniture. Don't work at a campus dining hall. Don't file papers at an office. These jobs will be distracting, demanding of your time, and energy draining. Instead, **try to find a strategic job at your college.** One option is to get a paid position in an academic department in which you have an interest. Being a paid research assistant may still mean a lot of cleaning beakers or making photocopies, but at the same time you are immersed in academia. You will be working with professors and will become very familiar with their research projects. The step from being an assistant to getting more seriously involved with a professional research project is much easier than trying to do the same thing as just another random student. And you will be creating valuable faculty connections. This type of strategic job provides both money and a head start toward succeeding at college.

Another option is to obtain one of your college's many fluff jobs, which include any position that involves sitting in a quiet space while doing a minimum of actual work. This usually means manning an information desk at a library or similar campus building, though other jobs in this category include being a music monitor (i.e., handing out practice room keys) or working the reception desk at an out-of-the-way campus organization. The wonderful benefit of these jobs is that they act as enforced study halls. If you have to sit at a quiet desk, virtually undisturbed, for two to three hours, you basically have no other option but to study or otherwise slowly die from boredom. These jobs can be a great way to add some structure and consistency to your schoolwork.

The secret to obtaining any desirable position at your college is to inquire about openings early. Very early. Start contacting the individuals in charge of the job you want at least a month before the semester begins. Manning an info desk is not exactly neuroscience, so getting hired is more about being the first to ask than any other criteria. A paid research assistant position is a little more difficult to obtain. However, by contacting the department early and showing real enthusiasm, your chances of getting hired are greatly increased. Your faculty adviser, and other connections from the professorial ranks, can also be helpful here.

When it comes to student employment, the bottom line is that unless you have some sort of extraordinary skill, you are going to be paid around $7 an hour no matter what you do. If the money is the same for every potential job, then you might as well find a position that best helps your academic career. You are not at college to build professional work experience; you are there to become a successful student. Make your job an asset, not an obstacle, on the way to meeting your goals.

# 41

## Use Three Days to Write a Paper

*There are two* types of papers assigned at college: long ones and short ones. Long papers are typically of the research variety. They require quite a bit of time to complete because you have to track down sources, generate original theses, and master complicated new ideas. These papers are really hard. Sorry! (See Rule #4, "Start Long-Term Projects the Day They Are Assigned," for some guidance on how to make them less difficult.) Fortunately, the vast majority of papers assigned at college are short papers. These range from actually being short (2–4 pages), to being not so short (5–10 pages), to being downright evil (11–20 pages). Whatever the length, the defining features of a short paper are that you typically have only a week or two to write them, and they usually deal with material you covered in class and your readings (not original re-

101

search). These papers are the bread and butter of a typical liberal arts curriculum. You need to master them.

**A good rule is to always use three days to write your short papers.** This doesn't mean spending three days working on the paper; it means spending three days actually writing. Before your fingers first hit the keyboard, you need to finish any necessary preparation. Go back through your readings and notes and figure out what you want to say. Make an outline of your points, write out your thesis with crystal-clear clarity, and have the sources you need to quote readily available. This is the easy part. Preparing information for a paper is much less painful than actually writing. And for a short paper you are not covering anything you haven't seen before, so this prep work can be accomplished in one or two sittings.

Once you have your ideas and materials organized, it's time to spend three days writing. That's right, three. The first day is the hardest. If possible, make the first day a weekend day, or a weekday when you don't have many obligations. On this first day try to power through your outline and build a rough draft of the entire paper. Get all of your ideas written down. This first draft will take a while to write as you will be consuming and organizing a lot of thoughts all at once. It will also be long. Probably much longer than your assigned page limit. Don't worry; its length will be brought back under control shortly. Also, don't worry about crafting perfect prose, you will fix all of that later. Just get all of your ideas down in some sort of a coherent manner.

Your second day should be much easier than your first. Go

back through your massive rough draft, tighten up your wording, cut out excess arguments, and add support where it seems to be glaringly missing. The goal of the second day is to pare your prose down into lean and mean arguments. No sentence should be wasted. Don't worry about the nitty-gritty details of fixing all grammatical mistakes and perfecting sentence structures. The second day is all about making your argument compelling.

Finally we come to the third day, which is the easiest. Make another run through your paper, this time really polishing the details of your arguments where they might still feel a little thin. Make sure all your support is clearly defined and advances your thesis. Check that all your sentences read well, that the ideas flow logically, and look for any remaining grammatical mistakes. Go back and rework your introduction and conclusion to make them exactly match the final form of your paper. Print out and edit your writing with a pencil at least twice. There is something about reading text on a computer screen that makes it easy to overlook stupid mistakes. Then, finally, go through and make sure your citations are properly formatted, add a cover sheet if needed, check your margins, and handle any other administrative details demanded by your professor.

All too often, students try to combine all three days into one. This is a horrible idea. It's painful to try to combine so much intense concentration into one drawn-out experience, and it produces lackluster papers. By approaching your paper fresh on two separate occasions after you complete your rough draft, you will really hone your arguments and produce the type of polished writing that can easily receive an A. Notice that this approach doesn't necessarily require much more time than the traditional approach (a one-day twelve-hour marathon of writing is equal to spending six hours the first day, four hours the second, and two hours the third), but it produces a much better result.

There is, however, one exception to the three-day rule. When working with the aforementioned "evil" papers (fifteen plus pages), three days may not be enough time, but the concept of breaking up the work into three chunks still applies. Just expand the size of these chunks. For example, for a really long paper you might stretch your rough-draft-writing phase out over three days, and the argument-polishing phase out over two days. What is important is preserving the idea of always separating the paper-writing process into three distinct segments.

Successful students don't spend much more time working than their peers, they just spend their working time smarter. Take three days to write your short papers—your mind, your body, and your professors will thank you.

# 42

## Don't Undersleep, Don't Oversleep

*If you had* a dollar for every time your parents told you that you need to get eight hours of sleep, I would ask you to lend me some money. It's common knowledge in the world of parental lore that children need eight hours of sleep to stay healthy. And, of course, parents never hesitate to tell us about this crucial observation; it's something they never grow tired of (pun, unfortunately, intended). I don't know if this sleep information is true, and truthfully it doesn't really matter. What is important is that you know how much sleep *you* need to remain energetic throughout the day. For some people that may be exactly eight hours. For others, such as me, it's more like seven hours. For a lucky few, four or five hours seem to work fine. If you want to succeed at college, you need to have energy and focus every single day. So figure out how much sleep you need so that you don't have to fight the siren call of your bed all afternoon.

Mix this with exercise and a healthy diet and you will have all the energy and focus necessary to function at a high level.

Now, here is the important part: **Once you have landed upon this magic number of sleep hours, keep it consistent.** This means not only should you avoid getting too few hours of sleep, you should also avoid getting too many hours of sleep. Sleeping-in wastes time in the morning that doesn't need to be wasted. And if you upset your sleep pattern with an aggressive disdain for your alarm clock, you can actually end up feeling more tired than if you had slept less. I know this is hard to hear as a college student, but the rule to follow is: The fact that you can sleep more, doesn't mean that you should.

Contrary to popular sentiments, maximizing sleep should not be your ultimate goal as a student. Sleep is just a tool to help you function. Treat your body like a machine—give it exactly what it needs to perform its best, not any more, not any less. Give the snooze button a rest. Try to sleep only the amount you need to make it through the day.

## 43

# Relax Before Exams

*True or false:* The final hour before an exam is a good time to frantically review your notes as you sprint across campus from classmate to classmate trying to reconfirm your understanding of hard concepts, all the while attempting to skim the various conclusions of a toppling stack of assigned books only to collapse into your seat mere moments before the exam is passed out? The answer is, most decidedly, false.

This period of time is more crucial than you might imagine. The typical college exam tests two things: your ability to demonstrate an understanding of complicated material, and your ability to recall and synthesize this information under pressure. It's not just what you know, but also how well you can explain what you know in short, hectic bursts. This means that after you put in the study time needed to learn the material, you have to put in the relaxation time needed to prepare your mind to operate under pressure. Some students believe it's beneficial to maintain "intellectual momentum" by studying right up until the testing begins. This is not true. Such an approach releases too much adrenaline, which makes you jittery and unfocused. The best state for your mind to be in is confident and calm. **Take the hour before an exam to relax.**

Think of it as an Olympic athlete would, training for the mile-run. In the weeks leading up to the competition the athlete trains hard. But on the day of the race, he rests and conserves his energy so that he can be ready to compete hard when the starting gun fires. Your studying is your training, and the hour before the exam is your prerace rest period.

Read a nonacademic book. Listen to music that makes you happy. Run a couple of errands. Have a conversation with a friend. Work on unrelated—nondemanding—schoolwork. The key is to keep your mind active and energized, but not exhausted. Then head over to the exam fifteen minutes early. On the way, start to lightly review some material that you feel particularly good about. Imagine yourself writing a strong essay on this topic, imagine the professor handing the class a copy of your essay as an example of a good answer. This technique is more than just shameless ego-stroking, it builds your confidence, and, more important, it warms up your mind in a good and controlled sort of way. When you arrive at the test location, avoid the temptation to frantically catalog all the concepts you are a little shaky on. Try to keep your mind blank, or, alternatively, continue thinking confidence-boosting thoughts about doing really well. When the exam is finally handed out, take a deep breath and have at it. You should be mentally nimble, rested, and energized by the time your pen hits the paper.

Most students neglect this psychological component of exams. To only study the material but not prepare your mind for the stress of the test-taking experience, means you are only partially prepared to do your best. Taking the time to relax and then to carefully reenergize right before an exam is a great way to consistently score well.

# 44

## Make Friends Your #1 Priority

*Perhaps I should* begin by explaining what this rule doesn't mean, lest some of you get the wrong idea. This rule doesn't mean that honing your video-game skills with your roommate should be your number one priority. This rule doesn't mean that making sure no friend ever watches TV alone should be your number one priority. And this rule doesn't mean that scheduling a dozen social encounters a day should be your number one priority. What it does mean is that you should never take your friends for granted. They are your social safety net. When you are having a bad day, when you do poorly on an exam, when you are rejected by a member of the opposite sex, or fall flat on your face attempting to walk up the library steps, your friends are the ones who will help you feel better. When you are bored or lonely, your friends will instill laughter and excitement and misadventure back into your routine. When you feel adrift and are unsure of where you fit in the world, your friends will prevent you from taking yourself too seriously. The experiences you have together will become some of your best stories for years to come. In short, **you cannot let a busy schedule come between you and your friendships.**

Striking a balance between work and friends is not that difficult. The key is to plan ahead. Arrange to have one meal with some friends almost every day (see Rule #28, "Eat Alone Twice a Day"). You can e-mail them in advance, or just ask buddies who live nearby on the way to the dining hall. You can also arrange to eat with one particular person at a certain time on a certain day each week. This can be a nice ritual, and a great way to keep social without having to expend much planning energy. But even if your dining schedules don't click, still keep in touch with your best friends on a daily basis. If you are busy, shoot them an e-mail to say hi and to see what's going on. If you have the time, swing by to see them in person. If a friend invites you to do something and you are not too busy, find the energy to go. If a friend invites you to do something, and you are really busy, don't go, but make plans to get together later in the week. Most important, if a good friend needs help, drop everything and go.

Making friends your number one priority doesn't mean sacrificing your other obligations, but it does demand that you keep them in mind. Friends are your most valuable asset at college. Fuel these friendships. Don't let other commitments and goals push them to the periphery of your life.

# 45

## Don't Binge Drink

*A lot of* college students drink. A lot of college students also consider "streaking" to be a respectable form of recreation, which is to say, just because a lot of students do something, doesn't mean it's necessarily logical. I'm not interested here in discussing the various arguments for and against drinking at college. Whether or not you choose to drink should be a decision based on your personal convictions, health history, and beliefs. But you do need to be aware of how alcohol affects your ability to perform as a student.

Going out and having a couple of drinks on a Friday or Saturday night might slow you down a little the next morning, but it's nothing a quart of Starbucks and a couple of Advil can't handle. However, if you go out and binge drink—that is, consume alcohol until your speech is slurred, your gait shaky, and your stomach nauseated—no latte in the world is going to perk you up the next morning, and you will have just lost an entire day of productivity. A serious hangover makes it impossible to accomplish what you need to accomplish, not to mention that it weakens your body in general, makes you more susceptible to sickness, and leaves you feeling downright miserable. You can drink and still win at college. But you can't regularly binge drink and expect to succeed. Be mature and make the right decisions to keep your mind and body in a condition to perform your best.

# 46

**Ignore Your Classmates' Grades**

*It has happened* to all of us at least once. A test is handed back, and you did pretty well, but then you notice that a classmate has left a copy of her test laying conspicuously, almost invitingly, visible on her desk. You take a quick look. She did better than you! If you typically do well in a particular class, seeing a better mark on someone else's test can be like receiving a quick kick to the gut. You cannot help but feel as if your classmate is smarter than you, and this is a bad feeling. When you lose your academic confidence in a course, you also lose your energy for that subject, you do the readings with less attention, you ask fewer questions in class, and you are easily rankled in future testing situations. But here's the kicker: all of this negativity happens for no good reason. Why? Because **different students' grades on any given test or paper are not directly comparable.**

For example, say you receive an 84 on a test and your class-mate receives a 93. Your initial instinct is to see her as the superior intellect, the one who had an easier time mastering the subject at hand. But imagine all the factors that could have gone into that 93. Maybe she just happened to focus her studying on a specific book or topic about which a lot of questions were asked on that particular exam. Maybe an unusually light schedule the week before gave her time to really log some long hours during her preparation. Maybe she bombed her last test so she put everything she had into knocking this one out of the ballpark. Maybe she just got more sleep the night before. The point is that there are too many factors that can account for both good and mediocre academic performance on any given day, and none of these factors has anything to do with intelligence.

So save yourself a lot of unjustified grief (or pride), and simply ignore your classmates' grades. Worry about your performance and progress; let your classmates worry about their own.

# 47

## Seek Out Phenomenal Achievers

*Success is relative.* Some students have modest ambitions. They would be happy to just land a decent job after graduation, or make the dean's list a couple of times. Other students pursue phenomenal dreams. They want to be a senator, start a major company, or get accepted into a world-class graduate program. As a student interested in becoming a standout, you should follow the example of this latter group, and define your notion of success to be as ambitious as possible. The bigger the goals you pursue, the more exciting the accomplishments you rack up along the way, and the more interesting your life becomes. **How do you upgrade your notion of personal success? One easy method is to seek out phenomenal achievers.**

What is a phenomenal achiever? Every school has them. It's

that rather nice math major who happens to be a Rhodes Scholar, NSF Graduate Fellowship winner, and author of a chapter in a calculus textbook. Or that quiet drama major who has already produced two plays, won a bevy of creative awards, and is working seriously on his first novel. Or that student assembly officer who just formed a statewide youth mentoring program, and works on national political campaigns during his off-terms. Find these people. Meet them. Treat them to a meal and have them spill their guts. Find out how they did what they did, what it felt like, and what they want to try next.

The idea here is to expose yourself to possibility. When you spend enough time talking to phenomenal achievers, two things happen. First, you will become inspired. The thought of accomplishing the sort of achievements that fill these student's résumés will pique your energy. Second, learning from the details of their endeavors, you begin to notice how the interests in your life could feasibly lead to similar accomplishments.

After you spend time with the math whiz, you might realize that you, too, could harness your academic talents to work on attention-grabbing projects with professors. A lunch with the young playwright might help motivate you to finally write that screenplay you have been thinking about. And a conversation with the student assembly officer might inspire you to take on a leadership role in community outreach programs on campus.

Spending time with phenomenal achievers is one of the most

effective ways to expand the scope of your ambitions. It's also a great way to interject excitement and inspiration into your life. Make a habit out of getting in touch with these people. And do it often. Soon you will be the person others come to with wide eyes and a host of admiring questions.

# 48

**Learn to Listen**

*One of the* most important skills to develop at college is the ability to really listen. Why? Well, there is no easy way to say this, but, as a college student, your opinion doesn't matter all that much. We all love to express our ideas and beliefs, and youthful confidence can make it tempting to jump right in and argue with a professor or other students. But in truth, **it's much more important that you spend your undergraduate years developing an ability to synthesize ideas and learn.**

This is not to say that you should never express your point of view. On the contrary, be it in class or just talking with friends, it can be a great learning experience to have constructive discussions or debates (the key word being "constructive"; arguing over who "sucks more" doesn't count). But here is the secret to being a good listener: Never be the first person to give an opinion. If you are in a group or talking with a professor, and a topic worthy of discussion comes up, you gain nothing by jumping right in and providing what seems to you to be the obviously correct opinion. You might be right, or you might be wrong, but who cares? This is an opportunity (a) to increase other people's esteem and respect for you, and (b) to learn. Instead of launching right into your beliefs, listen carefully to what the other people in the discussion think. Ask constructive questions as well. Develop a good understanding of their positions, repeating back parts of their argument to ensure that you have complete comprehension. Only then should you interject your own thoughts, and you should do so with careful aplomb. Which is a gentle way of saying don't start your retort with: "Welcome to wrong-answer-ville; population, You!" Instead, lay out the different takes on the subject—yours and theirs—and introduce the question of what points should be involved in evaluating which side is better.

For example, don't debate gun control by arguing about the danger of handguns. Instead, discuss your different interpretations of the second amendment and what strategies or historical examples of constitutional disputes can best help you reconcile your disagreement. The former will lead to a lot of righteous indignation and heated tempers, the latter will help both of you understand the issue with more clarity. You are probably never going to convince an opponent that they are wrong, so why waste time being dogmatic?

The beauty of this approach is that it works just as well in a classroom discussion of constitutional jurisprudence as it does when shooting the breeze with a friend. If you learn to listen, not only will you develop a much clearer understanding of issues that you care about, but you will also gain other people's respect.

A good listener at college is rare. Keep this rule in mind so you can be one of the few, the well respected, and the well informed.

# 49

**Never Pull an All-Nighter**

*It's inevitable, right?* Every once in a while your busy schedule will lead to a point where your have a big test to study for, or a paper to write, and there are only twelve hours left before the deadline. You then have no choice but to heroically work throughout the wee hours of the night, finishing the assignment just as the sun begins to rise. In short, sometimes even the best of us must pull an all-nighter. Wrong!

There are two main problems with pulling an all-nighter. First, after around two A.M., your mental ability is reduced to roughly that of a toaster oven. If you think that in the middle of the night your sleep-addled mind is going to form meaningful links to the material you are "studying," then you are sadly mistaken. The typical all-nighter turns into a painful stretch of mind-numbing stumbling through books and notes with the occasional burst of panic-induced focus. It may seem as if you are adding another five hours of work time by pushing through until dawn, but the reality is that you are more likely adding one hour of worthwhile work time and four hours of useless rambling. Is that really worth the pain?

The second problem is the aftereffects of an all-nighter. The following day you are a zombie. It's a horrible feeling. Your ability to successfully take a test, pay attention in a class, exercise, or do anything remotely productive is basically nonexistent. Recent research on rest and mental functioning has shown that when you are seriously sleep-deprived your brain activity is basically indistinguishable from that of someone who is fully asleep. Which, needless to say, is not a good state to be in when you are trying to perform academically. And not only will your all-nighter cost you the entire next day, it will probably also end up forcing you to bed much earlier than usual, disrupting your sleep pattern for more days to follow.

Why, then, do all-nighters remain common? Perhaps the biggest myth surrounding this classic collegiate study technique is that all-nighters are inevitable. Students about to partake in a late-night work marathon typically complain about how they "have no choice." They try to come across as very stoic and brave, academic warriors courageously facing an unavoidable battle. The reality, however, is that all-nighters are never inevitable. They only occur if you *decide* to start working the day before.

Here is the rather complicated and completely unexpected secret to avoiding this situation: **Don't decide to start working**

123

**the day before.** It's really that simple. When you know a test or a paper is coming up, schedule in advance the days you need to work on it. Then, on those days, give priority to this work. If you get only one thing done on the days leading up to a big deadline, make it your studying or writing first, and everything else later. Take staying up all night off your list of options. It should never be considered a viable approach for getting things done.

All-nighters are like poison for a successful student. With a little scheduling effort and the right priorities, you can avoid them altogether.

# 50

**Laugh Every Day**

*They say laughter* is the best medicine, and this holds especially true for college students, mainly due to one particularly nasty recurring problem: stress. College-related stress has a negative impact on the body. It leads to exhaustion, a decrease in metabolism, a weakened immune system, and general unhappiness. It's hard to avoid situations that cause stress, but it's not hard to find methods to combat its negative effects. Laughing is one of these methods.

Not to get too physiologically specific, but the act of laughing releases an antibody known as IgA. This little critter releases endorphins, fights off stress-related hormones, and in general makes you feel good. Not to mention the psychological benefits of letting loose. The physical act of smiling actually shifts your mental state toward the positive. Basically, laughing is like an ultra-powerful vitamin, and you should treat it as such.

**Find something every single day that will make you laugh.** It can be a conversation with some wisecracking friends, reading *The Onion,* or watching *The Daily Show with Jon Stewart* each night. Maybe you have a particular writer who makes you laugh (I challenge you to read Dave Barry or David Sedaris without cracking a smile), or maybe you get a kick out of well-formed, Web-based dementia like HomestarRunner.com. The point is that you need to make a conscious effort to seek out avenues of laughter each and every day. Life is short, and the physical and mental benefits of this simple activity are outstanding for something that is so enjoyable and easy to do.

126

# 51

## Use High-Quality Notebooks

*This rule is* absolutely essential. Without it, you have a zero percent
chance of ever graduating college. Okay, maybe not. It's not that a
low-quality notebook will be unable to meet your needs, but the
general concept of investing in your school supplies is surprisingly
important.

If you take notes in a cheap, frayed, spiral notebook—sometimes cramming several classes' notes into the same space to the
point where there is always a serious search necessitated before
you can ever find what you are looking for—this will impact your
retention of the material. When it comes time to review, this sloppy
presentation will make it difficult for your mind to successfully
structure the ideas, facts, and themes. Imagine instead that for
each class your notes are written on a high-quality notepad, with a
good solid pen, where every lecture is clearly dated and located in

proper order. This sense of quality and order helps you establish a serious mind-set. The information is laid out clearly and cleanly, and it's easily accessible so your mind is free to focus on synthesizing the concepts, not tracking them down.

This idea extends past notebooks, of course. In addition, you should buy one high-quality folder for each class. Keep all relevant paperwork for a particular class in its specific folder, and keep all of these folders in one specific place in your desk where they are consolidated and easy to access. Keep your class notebooks in an otherwise empty drawer. Use high-quality pens, mechanical pencils, and highlighters. When studying, buy a separate folder to hold all your review sheets, summarized notes, practice tests, and related material. You get the idea.

In general, making sure to use high-quality and well-organized school supplies is an important way to reduce the stress of disorganization. It also helps structure your course material in an efficient way, and creates the right mental cues for a serious student doing serious work. Using a high-quality notebook will not guarantee you success, but it will create the right environment for it to flourish.

## 52

## Keep a Work-Progress Journal

*There are some* students who have no problem working consistently   129
and seriously on long-term projects. In the week before the big
test, they review diligently for two hours every day; as a paper
deadline approaches they work on refining their words each afternoon until the final product shines. Good mood or bad, energetic
or lazy, busy or free, they easily accomplish what needs to be accomplished. We tend not to like these students very much. Because, of course, for most of us, working on a long-term project is
a stressful, grueling, horrible thing.

Starting these projects on the day they are assigned (see Rule
#4) is a great way to break the initial specter of procrastination. But
getting the ball rolling early is only half the battle. What happens
when you are feeling unusually tired on day four of the twelve days
you have scheduled to work on a big project? How does one fight

that insistent urge to put off the current day's work, convincing yourself that one lazy day won't make that much of a difference? Such a pattern can easily begin to repeat itself. You start skipping more and more scheduled study time, working only when you feel just right, and by the time the deadline approaches you realize that you are woefully behind where you need to be. All that hard work you put in to get started on time has now gone to waste. This happens to the best of us. To succeed on long-term projects you must recognize that most of the advantages of starting early are diminished if you don't work regularly once you have begun. This may seem dire, but it doesn't have to be.

If you have a hard time working consistently on long-term projects, the solution might be the use of a work-progress journal. The concept is simple. The human ego is a powerful force, and for a student trying to stay on top of big assignments, a little ego can be used to help keep you on track. Allow me to explain. You should buy a small spiral notebook that you store in your top desk drawer. Every night, follow the very simple habit of jotting down the day's date, the long-term work you had scheduled for the day, and the work that you actually accomplished. These entries should be very brief, no more than a line each. The idea is that the actual act of keeping the journal is very easy, so you should have no problem making it an unbreakable habit.

This little act of recording any discrepancy between work scheduled and work accomplished is amazingly effective in keeping your mind in the game. The reason it seems so easy to ignore long-term work obligations is because no one holds you accountable. However, the thought of having to record in your journal that you "accomplished none of the day's scheduled work," introduces a degree of accountability into your life. No one wants a permanent record of their temporary laziness, so you'll sigh loudly, pour another cup of coffee, and grind out what needs to get done.

A work-progress journal is a simple concept and easy to execute, but the effect on your productivity is surprisingly profound. By holding yourself accountable you can do a much better job of managing your time and sticking to your schedules.

# 53

**Seek Out Fun**

*Contrary to what* you may have seen in every college movie ever made, as a student you probably will not find yourself humorously falling into one crazy adventure after another. It's of course important that you have a lot of fun at college. Student antics are a great way to strengthen friendships, keep your mood light, and build up a whole collection of stories that one day you can make sure never, ever to tell your children. However, **if you don't actively seek out fun, it won't actively seek out you.**

For a freshman, the thought of missing out on fun activities may seem nonsensical. The first year of college is traditionally defined by all sorts of wild high-jinks, new faces, and exploration of your new surroundings. But as you move on through your collegiate career, and your schedule becomes more and more packed with more serious activities and obligations, it can become easy to let weeks and weekends pass by with no real excitement. And this is sad. When you lose the positive benefits of letting loose on a regular basis, you are much more susceptible to developing a disgruntled mind-set, a loathing for your studies, and a general state of unhappiness. This is why the dreaded Sophomore Slump is often preceded by the arrival of a suddenly packed sophomore schedule that drastically reduces time for impromptu fun.

The key to avoiding this tedious fate is to actively plan unpredictability and adventure into your life. This may seem a little counterintuitive, but it works, and it's better than the alternative. Gather groups of friends to make a circuit of weekend room-parties, buy outfits for a themed frat party, take road trips with ill-defined directions, see movies at odd times, track down random area landmarks that are only rumored to exist, visit the local bars you have never been to, invite out new people, throw parties yourself, and best of all, perpetrate epic pranks. When unplanned adventure leaves your life, replace it with planned adventure. Seek out fun, and your college experience will be greatly enhanced.

133

# 54

## Inflate Your Ambition

134    *While it may* be true that good things come to those who wait, it's also true that extraordinary, head-turning things come to those who say "screw waiting!" and just go for it. Take a moment to inventory the various pursuits you have going on. How many of these goals would make you a standout if accomplished? How many would cause a professor to mention you, unprompted, at a faculty meeting? How many would lead to your name being brought up for award nominations? If you answered "none," then it's time to inflate your ambition.

Of course, needless to say, college is all about trying new things and building up a variety of different experiences—and that's okay. But the difference between a successful student and a regular student is that the former is always on the lookout for situations where they can really push a talent to its limits. This is the essence of inflating your ambition. **Take the most important projects or commitments with which you are involved, and pump up your criteria for success.**

For example, say you're an education major, and you have set your sights on the respectable goal of trying to do as well as possible in your classes. You could inflate your ambition by becoming an undergraduate grader for an intro class, working hard at obtaining feedback from the students, and then at the end of the term talking with the professor about ways in which the class projects could be updated or improved. This would likely be exciting and enjoyable for you, not to mention impressive. Or maybe you're a biology major working as a research assistant. You could inflate your ambition by deciding on your own to create an easy-to-use bibliographic database to help the principal researchers put together their citations. Or you could sacrifice a weekend to set up a system to automatically generate the charts that were otherwise slotted to be accomplished piece by piece over the next couple of weeks. That certainly would turn heads.

Inspiring, interesting students always seem to be defying the norm. You don't need to bog yourself down with an oppressive number of activities and commitments; instead, just take your reasonable slate of existing goals and take them to the next level. It's not that hard to inflate your ambition, but few ever think to do it. It's a critical skill to learn for anyone interested in becoming a standout.

135

# 55

## Get Involved with Your Major Department

**136**   *A collegiate academic* department is like a small corporation. At the

top of the hierarchy are the professors, who are supported by

dozens of assistants and administrators all working toward the

same two goals: to create an environment where the professors

have the resources they need to publish and advance knowledge in

their fields; to help train qualified students to go out into the world

and herald the department's reputation. It's this second goal that

most directly affects you.

Your department wants you to be involved so they can help

you succeed beyond your undergraduate career. This is why once

you officially declare your major, you will begin to receive notices

for a wide variety of events sponsored by your department. These

include pragmatic talks on subjects like choosing your course load,

writing an undergraduate thesis, and preparing for the job world or graduate school. These also include lectures given by leaders in the field, seminars conducted by professors, graduate students' public thesis defenses, corporate recruitment sessions, and yes, even parties. In the chaos of classes, extracurricular activities, and a healthy social schedule, these optional events are easy to avoid. **Don't avoid them.**

You need to get involved with your major department. Showing up at optional events and becoming a recognized face among the faculty is a way to do this. The recommendations and personal contacts you need for your future will come mainly from professors in your major department, so they need to know you. They need to enjoy your company. They need evidence of your involvement in their domain. This doesn't mean you have to show up at every single departmental event—that might seem a little . . . what's the word? . . . oh, yeah, *obsessive*. But you must make a point of showing up to something about once a month. And when you run into professors at these events, have something brief (and interesting) to say. You can talk about a paper they just published, ask a question about a class they offer, or simply comment on the weather. These little interactions will help solidify these important relationships.

This strategy is of course no substitute for getting substantively involved in your field of study (see Rule #20, "Jump into Research as Soon as Possible.") or building particularly close bonds with one or two individual professors (see Rule #8, "Befriend a Professor"), but it's the icing on the cake in terms of setting yourself up to receive the full support of your department.

# 56

## Care About Your Grades, Ignore Your G.P.A.

**138**

*While at college* you will run into some students with an alarming concern for the impact of every single graded assignment on their overall academic standing. These are the students who develop spreadsheets to instantly calculate how many thousandths of a point the B+ on their last organic chemistry test will nudge their cumulative G.P.A. Some people call these students pragmatic. I call them weird.

Does a standout student get good grades? Sure, for the most part. They study smart and engage the material, so they tend to do well. But what is more important is that they treat each class as an intellectual challenge to conquer. Sometimes things don't turn out the way they want, and this is unavoidable. It's easy to write a good paper but touch on the wrong topics. Or to fly through a big math problem with ease but use the wrong algorithm. Bad grades happen, and this shouldn't be a big deal. As long as you put in the effort, who cares about one bad day?

I once met a particularly awe-inspiring Rhodes Scholar who delighted in telling the story of how she bombed her final exam in a calculus course. Did this disaster ruin her academic career? Not at all. She may have made some dumb mistakes on one test, but in the end, she made sure she eventually conquered those concepts. In fact, the first step she took after her ill-fated exam was to head straight to her professor's office hours. She went over the exam with him in detail, separating dumb mistakes from actual misunderstandings and discussing the right answers until she felt in control of the material. She demonstrated so much enthusiasm for the subject that the professor invited her back to be a teaching assistant the next semester, even though her grade in the class wasn't anywhere near the A- usually required for becoming a T.A. The point is that she didn't care about getting a bad grade. Her concern was with understanding the material. This focus on learning for the sake of learning, not for the sake of grades, may not have made her Valedictorian, but it did propel her to a diverse and exciting collegiate career—not to mention quite a few national awards and honors.

If you begin to obsess about your G.P.A., much of the excitement of college is lost. Every test stops being an opportunity to show off your ability to engage the material, and instead becomes a potential devastation to your overall academic standing. Every paper stops being an exercise in crafting words, and instead creates recurring fear that you might have come to the wrong conclusion. And at the end of every term you will exist in a state of nervous apprehension as you wait for your final grades to be released. In short, obsessing about your G.P.A. makes your life stressful and can derail you from your larger goals.

**If you want to be a successful student, forget about your G.P.A.** Ignore it. Don't talk about it. Make no attempt to know the numbers. You should approach your collegiate career with confidence and energy. Use the rules in this book to perform your best. When you have the occasional academic misstep, never look back, just move on. Life is too short to demand perfection from yourself. Feel free to care about your grade when you are preparing for a specific project, test, or paper, but ignore your overall G.P.A.

## 57

## Always Go to Class

*The following are* not valid excuses for skipping class: I'm really
tired; I feel a little congested; the lecture notes are online; I have
other work that I need to catch up on; I don't want to miss the
morning's third episode of *Blue's Clues* on Nickelodeon. The following *are* valid excuses for skipping class: I have a fever of 105 de-
grees; I need to fly to L.A. to accept an Academy Award; today in
class we are reviewing a book *I* wrote; my leg is caught in a bear
trap. The moral of this exercise: **Always go to class!**

Lectures are the source of the most important material covered by any class. The professor is telling you what he or she feels
is necessary to know about a subject, what is not necessary to know
about a subject, and what is the right way to approach, analyze, or
discuss a subject. The best way to engage this important material
is for you to be surrounded by your peers, sitting in a lecture hall,

the professor at the blackboard, and you asking questions when you don't fully understand topics. In short, you need to be there.

Attending class is not the same as reviewing the PowerPoint slides you downloaded from the Internet, or going through the barely legible notes of a friend. The specific cadence of the professor's speech, how he or she structures and clarifies the information during the lecture, the collective answers to the questions asked during class, these are all important elements to helping you cement an understanding of this crucial material.

In addition, it does wonders for your academic confidence to attend class. Skipping a lecture is like skipping a gym workout: you will feel guilty, behind, and lazy. This lack of confidence, coupled with a lack of first-person exposure to the most important material in your class, is going to lead to poor academic performance, and this will cause your confidence to spiral even lower. Avoid the descent by making this rule nonnegotiable. If you skip class for no good reason, even once, attendance for every class suddenly becomes debatable. Don't make this an argument that you have to win every morning. Always go to class.

## 58

## Set Arbitrary Deadlines

*Students are good* at meeting looming deadlines. If you know something is due the next day, you can usually marshal your resources,
sharpen your focus, and grind out the work that needs to be done.
However, once deadlines are moved further into the future, our
ability to assess and allocate work time is greatly diminished. In
fact, when a deadline is not immediate, our assessment of what
work should be done in the near future almost inevitably defaults
to "none."

"If this paper isn't due for another ten days, it's not like I have
to work on it right now." "It would be nice if I started researching
this afternoon, but it's not absolutely necessary, so why bother?" "If
that final project is three weeks from being due, there is really no
good reason why I shouldn't be watching TV."

These are the insidious thoughts that pervade the mind of a

student when a deadline seems harmlessly far away. This is why you need to force yourself to always be scheduling your time as if a deadline is near. The key to doing this: **Set arbitrary deadlines.**

This technique is simple in concept and surprisingly effective in practice. When you have a long-term project to work on, establish from the outset several nonnegotiable intermediate deadlines. Nothing is actually due on these deadlines, but they will exist as a nearby landmark to help you focus on near-term goals. The positive effect is powerful. Imagine the mental difference between having a paper due in three weeks, and having three days to solidify a thesis statement. Or imagine the difference between having a month to finish a big computer science programming project and having five days to build the user interface component. The former is daunting and invites procrastination, the latter is approachable and motivating.

This is not about tricking yourself into thinking you have something due when no actual deadline exists. It's about breaking large projects into smaller, short-term goals you can easily accomplish. By setting arbitrary deadlines, you blur the distinction between small and large assignments, and turn your schedule into one manageable flow of many small tasks. This is a fundamentally smarter way to handle your work.

144

# 59

**Eat Healthy**

*For many people,* one of the best things about going off to college is that they gain complete freedom in terms of what they eat. This means you can grab a slice of pizza from the dining hall for lunch, order a pizza for dinner, heat up leftover pizza for breakfast, and microwave personal pizza pockets for a mid-morning snack. While this sounds like fun, there are a few obvious reasons to avoid eating this way. First, you will gain weight, which is depressing and bad for your general health. Second, if you eat only junk food you will eventually get scurvy and die. Which is almost as bad as gaining extra weight. From the perspective of trying to succeed at college, **the most important reason to eat healthy is to maximize your energy.** Fatty foods, refined sugar, and large amounts of refined carbohydrates will all lead you to becoming increasingly sluggish. If you have ever tried to concentrate after

145

downing a Philly cheese steak or a bag of Doritos, you understand the danger of unhealthy foods. On the other hand, eating a non-fried chicken dish with vegetables, a serving of fruit, and a lot of water will energize you for hours. Eating healthy food is like adding premium fuel to your car; eating unhealthy food is like pulling the parking brake while you're still in motion.

Of course, it would be unreasonable to insist that you always eat extremely healthy foods without exception. We are only human. How many times can you resist the aroma of freshly sizzling hamburgers wafting from the grill, or ignore the fact that dorm delivery of steaming hot nachos is only one phone call away? There is nothing wrong with these periodic bursts of culinary slumming, but make them the exception, not the rule.

One effective method for managing your nutrition is to designate weekends as a time to eat what you want. During the school week, when you are attending classes, studying, and working on assignments daily, make a habit of treating your meals as nothing more than fuel. When the weekend rolls around, feel free to enjoy your meals more. If you have a hankering for pizza, fulfill it. If fries are calling your name, answer. Then, when Monday arrives, go back to thinking of your meals as simply a source of energy. Doing so will keep you energized, healthy, and happy.

*Doing volunteer work* is a great contribution to your community. 147
Every college offers a variety of programs, from peer mentoring to
Habitat for Humanity–style service projects, to fund-raising for
charities, to organizing education outreach efforts. The benefit of
community service is clear: you are helping people in need. This is
a noble thing to do, and students are generally a segment of soci-
ety with enough idealism and enthusiasm to actually make these al-
truistic efforts a part of their life. So make it a part of yours. Not
only is it important to get perspective on the world beyond the
confines of college, but it's good for your soul to dedicate time to
improving the lives of others. **But don't just volunteer, volunteer quietly.**

　　If you want to really derive the full personal benefit from your
community service work, don't talk about it much. Don't gripe to

your friends about the time commitment, don't work your generosity into conversations with others, and don't dwell on your involvement in job interviews. In short, keep the experience personal. When you volunteer quietly you are purifying your motivations. To be helping people without the benefit of outside praise and validation is a wonderful way to increase your sense of self-worth, strengthen your identity, and solidify your core values. These are traits that will carry you far in life. Do some good in the world for no other reason than wanting to be a part of the solution. It will redefine your approach to life for the better.

# 61

## Write as if Going for a Pulitzer

*College students do* a lot of writing, and this writing often deals with

subjects we don't really care much about (think "The Influence of

Constantinian Rome on the Carolingian Empire"), a situation that

leads to some bad habits. Chief among these is the tendency to

view writing as only the mechanical process of transferring infor-

mation from your head into grammatically correct sentences on

paper. Your work is good if you express all the right points; your

work is bad if you leave out information. Students tend to focus on

the substance of what they want to say, not on how they say it.

And this is a problem.

Good writing sparkles, not just in content but also in form.

When you read good writing, the varied rhythm of the sentences,

the careful choice of words, and the descriptive phrases grab your

attention and pull you through the topic toward inevitable conclusions. The experience is almost cinematic. You lose yourself in the prose and come out on the last page feeling as if you just experienced something significant. This is how you should aspire to write. A student who goes beyond just demonstrating coherent knowledge of a subject, and also artfully crafts the delivery, is going to stand out among his or her peers. Professors' eyes will light up, your name will be remembered, and you will score consistently higher on your written assignments.

One good way to remember to focus on form as well as content is to **approach every paper as if you were trying to win a Pulitzer Prize for explanatory reporting.** This prize is given each year to a work that "illuminates a significant and complex subject, demonstrating mastery of the subject, lucid writing and clear presentation." If you have any doubt as to what it means to illuminate a complex subject with lucid writing and clear presentation, go to www.pulitzer.org and read the recent winners in this category. These articles typically move deftly from anecdote, to question, to theory, then back again, pulling you deep into the core issues surrounding the issue at hand. They do this without ever getting bogged down in an overabundance of details or an oppressively didactic tone. This should be your model.

Be it a history paper, a biology thesis, or even a long e-mail to a professor, approach your writing as if you are trying to create an experience for your reader. Once you know what you want to say, shift your energy to develop an engaging way to say it. If you get bored when proofreading your work, you are not paying enough attention to your structure and style.

There is a hidden advantage to this mind-set that goes beyond superior academic performance. When you write as if going for a Pulitzer, the process becomes less painful. This may seem contradictory at first, but it is absolutely true. Writing is still hard, and it always will be, but it's exciting to craft an engaging passage, or use a particularly novel sentence structure, or build a paragraph around an interesting rhetorical rhythm. It puts creativity back into your work. You look forward to having someone read it. It adds an element of flair to what otherwise would be an entirely tedious process.

Few students follow this approach for writing, and their academic experience and performance suffers because of it. Be one of the few who can make even the Carolingian Empire seem engaging, and you will become a standout.

# 62

## Attend Political Rallies

152 *There was a* time when college campuses were ground zero for important activism in this country. During the Vietnam War, events like the Kent State shootings, classroom walkouts, and takeovers of administrative buildings helped define civil unrest in a war-weary country. Students helped fuel the idealistic campaigns of John F. Kennedy and his brother Robert. And students fed the flames of gender and racial equality battles. These were exciting times to be politically active on a college campus. Nowadays, it seems like the closest students get to activism is signing a petition to buy a frozen yogurt machine for the Student Union. We just don't care as much as we used to, and this is unfortunate.

Political activism is important. It speaks to your inherent idealism, it gives you a sense of purpose, and it elevates your sense of self-worth as you begin to realize that you can have an impact. To

CAL NEWPORT

become active in a cause is a powerful strategy for helping you feel fulfilled at college.

Fortunately, political activism is not entirely dead for Young America. Political rallies do still occur with some frequency on college campuses. Candidates march into lecture halls to make stump speeches, groups organize to debate issues, and the school administration is still occasionally challenged when their behavior strays from what students think is appropriate. People involved with these activities may be in the minority on your college campus, but don't let that stop you. Join this minority. Attend political rallies or protests. Stay in touch with controversial issues affecting both your college and the world as a whole. Identify which causes are important to you, and don't hesitate to demonstrate this support. Your student years represent a rare segment of your life span when you are intelligent enough to understand complicated issues, but young enough to still fully embrace an idealistic view of the world. Take advantage of this time while you have it, and get involved.

Attend political rallies and keep the flame of progressive thinking alive in American students, including you.

**Maximize Your Summers**

*Summer is a* great time to explore your interests free from the burden of academics. But just so there is no misunderstanding here, there is a difference between seriously exploring your interests and watching daytime television in your pajamas while eating Captain Crunch straight from the box. This is an important reality for any student interested in succeeding at college: **Summer vacation is not really a vacation.** Instead, it should be viewed as an annually occurring grace period when you get to put classes aside for two months and fully focus on nonacademic ambitions and experiences.

Start planning your summer in January, right after the holiday break. This may seem unnecessarily early, but there are quite a few exciting summer opportunities that have deadlines around February and March, and it takes time to organize your applications. Waiting until the last minute to find a summer job or activity is a plan almost always doomed to fall short of your expectations. The earlier you begin looking, the more interesting opportunities will be open to you.

What specifically should you do over the summer? The first major question you must answer is: to work, or not to work? Many students need to work over the break to build up the cash reserves necessary to afford a school year of pizza delivery, overpriced textbooks, and, how shall I put this discreetly, recreational liquid refreshments. However, this doesn't get you off the hook. If you start looking early you can very likely find a good-paying job that is also interesting. Don't head back to the same waitress gig or retail clerk position you held throughout high school. Instead, locate a position relevant to your interests and studies. These jobs can take the form of an official paid internship, a part-time job at an interesting place, a research assistant gig, or an unofficial paid position you create yourself. If you are a budding writer, try for as many paid publication internships as possible and, failing that, look for small jobs at local publications. (You would be surprised how many small-town newspapers are in need of a general-use intern/copy-editor to lighten the load.) If you are a biology major, inquire at every lab of every university and research institution within a twenty-mile radius of your home as to whether they have a lab assistant job available. If Grisham is your Shakespeare, personally contact two dozen different law firms to attest your dedication for

155

gaining a summer internship. Your advisers at college are another good source of both ideas and connections for interesting opportunities, so keep them in the loop as well.

If you don't need to make money over the summer, it's even more vital that you find a way to maximize your break, as few things look worse on a résumé than big open holes between June and August. In addition to the type of paid positions mentioned above, there is a whole other category of interesting unpaid positions that are oftentimes even easier to obtain. Search all the big names in your field of interest for internship positions, and if they don't offer any such positions, write a letter suggesting a program of your design. In this letter, make it clear why your presence would help the institution or company in question. This initiative goes a long way in selling your services. You can also consider the option of shadowing someone. This is a little-known technique that is often used to great effect by winning students. To shadow is to contact an inspiring, powerful person in a position relevant to your interests and to ask to spend some time observing them in action each week. You should explain that your rationale for shadowing him or her is to move closer toward your life passion by immersing yourself in his or her industry; you want to learn the life lessons of the pros. This technique is unusual, inspiring, and a great source of connections. However, if you go the route of shadowing, you also have to do your homework, know everything there is to know about this person and his or her company, and demonstrate a real

156

passion and dedication. Otherwise you will just be wasting someone's valuable time.

Finally, if there are any particular projects or talents that play a major role in your life, summer can be a great time to develop them. The key is to work such a personal pursuit into an official structure that includes accountability. If you want to spend the summer writing, do so with the goal of submitting works to three different competitions come fall. If you want to polish a musical talent, join a performance group, book some gigs, or organize a program to teach music to local kids. If you are a skilled computer programmer, work on contributing a clever piece of computer code to an Open Source project.

Few students expend the effort necessary to search out a great plan for their summers. If you put in the time to maximize your break, not only will you gain great experience, but you will also come across as a self-motivated standout in a sea of your lounging peers. Twelve hours of nightly sleep, bad daytime TV, and frequent movie rentals becomes tedious rather quickly. So take advantage of your summer to become a more interesting, inspired, and ambitious individual.

# 64

## Choose Goals, Explore Routes

*In this book* there are many rules suggesting that you pursue ambitious goals in your life. This is really important advice. It's this love of the excitement that surrounds ambitious projects that separates a standout student from a grind. Standout students are inspired, they are constantly looking to invent better ways of accomplishing goals, and they chase down head-turning opportunities because they can't imagine life without that thrill. Grinds, on the other hand, sacrifice everything for grades. Extracurricular ambitions merely rob them of studying time, they would rather work harder than smarter, and they are typically about as inspired as a doorstop. You don't want to be a grind. You do want to follow ambitious paths.

The act of pursuing goals, however, is not trivial. Once you set your mind to an ambitious project, how do you make that dream a reality? One of the most common mistakes you can make is to remain inflexible in your pursuits. Take for example the history major who is determined to get involved with original research before graduation. One approach she might take is to meet with each of her favorite professors and see if they have any need for a research assistant. This is a good plan, but what happens if they all claim to not need any help at the moment? Should she remain persistent on this tack, contacting those professors every semester to see if the situation has changed? This is one possible path, but there is still a good chance that it could be a dead end.

What our fictional student should do instead is to immediately branch out and try multiple, related paths. She could heavily investigate upcoming grant and scholarship deadlines for student research support. She could become heavily involved in writing research reviews and publishing minor original work for undergraduate journals related to social science. And she could seek off-term positions in nearby colleges or think tanks where she could be exposed to research. With such a varied approach, our student's chances of reaching her original goal become much more probable.

This is a key concept for succeeding with ambitious pursuits: **Once you have decided on a destination, explore many routes to get you there.** And once you begin exploring many routes, combine the approaches that seem successful, discard the attempts that fail, and constantly take the time to reevaluate what new opportunities may have just become recently available.

Trying to predict the full path that will eventually help you achieve your goals is often impossible. Using this technique is a smart way to maximize your chances for success.

## 65

## Don't Take Breaks Between Classes

*It's probably no* surprise to hear that once you enter college, your          161
educational experience will no longer be conducted in seven-hour
continuous stretches of back-to-back classes. Depending on how
your school handles its semester system, you will probably never
have more than three classes on most days. This means you will frequently be faced with long stretches of time in-between class periods. It might be ten minutes, or it might be a couple of hours, but
in an environment where scheduling is crucial, how you handle this
break time is important. Here is a common temptation: You get out
of a tiring morning class. You have an hour until your next class
starts at noon. This seems like a good time to relax with some TV,
and maybe even catch a quick catnap or three, because you would
be too rushed and tired to do anything productive in such a small
little time frame, right? As reasonable as this may sound, it's dead

wrong. Here is what you should do: **Don't take breaks between classes!**

There is a good reason for this rule, and it has everything to do with momentum. When you first drag yourself out of bed in the morning it's a struggle to get going. However, a strong cup of coffee, a big bowl of Cinnamon Toast Crunch, and a brisk walk to class will get your motor running. As your first class proceeds, your mind wakes up more and more. You are interacting with other students, you are trying to understand your professor's lecture, you are hoping to catch the attention of that cute girl (or handsome guy) in the second row—your momentum for the day is starting to build.

However, if after this first class you head home and pursue some serious relaxation, your momentum will grind to a halt. Now you have to start all over again with your next class. And if you take another intraclass break, you'll need to start over yet again. The problem here is that you only have so much energy on any given day, and you can't afford to waste it by repeatedly trying to remotivate yourself. You need, instead, to adopt a smart strategy for handling breaks between classes.

Use this time to keep active and to accomplish tasks that need to get done. Don't give your mind the chance to begin shutting itself back down. But don't overtax yourself either. A short break between classes is probably not a good time to pursue serious schoolwork. Unless you have more than an hour to kill, the context is too rushed for you to establish the concentration you need to accomplish worthwhile academic endeavors. Instead, use this time to take care of some chores. Before you head off to your first class, make a list of small tasks and errands you want to complete that day—buy toothpaste, stop by office hours, mail letters. This way you can keep your momentum building by rolling right out of class and straight into the chores you need to get done. If it's at all possible, try to avoid returning to your dorm room altogether; there are too many distractions there. You can use public computers and study spaces near your classrooms to accomplish any actual schoolwork or e-mailing you have planned.

This concept of maintaining your momentum throughout the morning and afternoon is simple but effective. When you hit the evening study hours, you want to do so energized and already finished with the day's smaller responsibilities.

163

# 66

**Don't Network**

164　*Networking is the* act of purposefully expanding your circle of acquaintances so that one day you can call upon these "friends" to put in a good word for you when the time is right. This skill has long been a staple of the professional business world. Personal connections between captains of industry add civility to the otherwise harsh world of corporate competition, and when it comes to hiring a new employee, a personal recommendation is worth a dozen glowing résumés. This being said, as far as you are concerned: **Leave networking to business professionals.** If you actively try to network as a college student you will annoy people. It's obnoxious. And you will not gain much more than disdain for your efforts.

　　Networking works best when it is an arrangement of mutual

benefit. If I work in the telecommunications industry, and you work in the Internet services industry, I would want to meet you. Your line of work is relevant to mine, it would serve me well to learn about what you do, and there are dozens of potential avenues in which our two companies might one day work together.

Now let's say that instead I work in the telecommunications industry, and you are a college student. I probably don't care about you. This is a pragmatic decision because there is no mutual benefit here. You want a job. There is no doubt of your goal. As a student there is really no other reason why you would be proactively trying to meet me, and quite frankly giving out jobs to recent graduates is not all that exciting. Unless I am a recruiter, you can't offer me anything I want, and your motives will be transparent. There is very little to gain from being the kid who goes to shake some guest lecturer's hand, asks him a softball question, and then embarrassingly tries to force highlights from his résumé into the conversation.

This is not to say that you should avoid making connections; you just have to find a better approach. One such approach is to *antinetwork*. Antinetworking is the art of getting what you want by never coming close to asking for it. This technique is simple and almost paradoxically effective.

When you first interact with a potential connection, his or her defenses will be high. "Here comes another student, better get ready for another thinly veiled attempt to request job help." The key is to act as if you have already been offered your dream job, and looking for employment is the farthest thing from your mind. You are confident, your future is secure, but you are curious about what this person does and why. This is the sole reason why you are talking to that visiting journalist, CEO, or research scientist. You ask insightful questions that show a solid understanding of the contact's work and a desire on your part to become more knowledgeable. You never once offer up elements of your résumé unless specifically asked, and even then, you do so with restraint. You show consideration and respect. You are confident without coming across like a used-car salesman. Not once do you show even a hint of underlying self-interest. In fact, you might even forget to give your name, leaving the contact to ask you as you walk away. This is antinetworking, and it works. Pleasantly surprised, the person you are talking to will drop their defenses, and, in the best of circumstances, remember the engaging student whose palpable enthusiasm and knowledge of the topic impressed them.

Now comes the hard part: How do you turn these isolated communications into a lasting connection? The best you can do is periodically send an update e-mail asking a very well-formed relevant question or requesting a thoughtful and relevant piece of advice. But never once ask for a blatant favor. The key to the antinetworking approach is to impress without imploring. The goal is that one day the contact, who has grown fond of you and is impressed by you and your integrity, will notify you that he or she knows of a job opening, and will be willing to recommend you if you are interested.

As a student it's the best you can do. It's hard, and it works infrequently. But transparent networking will work even less frequently, and you will end up annoying quite a few important people. Don't network. But keep your connections strong.

# 67

## Publish Op-Eds

*The Op-Ed pages* are by far the most entertaining section of any student newspaper. There is the second-year history major explaining how to solve world strife, the fourth-year government major lecturing on why he knows more about international diplomacy than the president's national security adviser, the third-year economics major confronting her anguish over whether to become a rich investment banker or an urban schoolteacher, the first-year English major exalting the joys of college in the fall, and, of course, the backward-baseball-cap-wearing fraternity brother who is not quite sure what year he is decrying the fact that no one "rages" anymore. The Op-Ed pages really are so much fun. They can make you laugh, they can make you angry, and sometimes they can even make you think. They are a forum for student voices, and even if the writing is often stilted, there is little denying the energy that surrounds them. Why not inject some of this energy into your student life?

**Write an Op-Ed piece once every semester.** Choose a topic you know a lot about, polish your prose and arguments, and aim to make a difference in the minds of your fellow students. Make your piece controversial if you want. There is a thrill to seeing your ideas published for all to read. There is an even bigger thrill to seeing letters to the editor and rebuttal pieces start to form a dialogue based on your seedling of an idea. It connects you to the rest of the student community, enhances your idealism, and inflates your sense of purpose. These traits will no doubt sound familiar, as they come up again and again in this book as being vital characteristics of a successful student. You don't have to offer up perfect, award-winning prose. Be radical, come out swinging and catch the readers off-guard, highlight issues that have never been mentioned, exude passion. The student newspaper is not the *Wall Street Journal*. You can get away with a lot and still have a good time doing it.

Write an Op-Ed piece at least once a term. There is no other experience quite like it. However, whatever you do, try to avoid waxing poetic about how no one "rages" at your school anymore—that's just plain embarrassing.

# 68

## Use a Filing Cabinet

170 *If you are* standing up right now you should probably sit down before reading any further. The rule that follows is so controversial and so shocking that it might disorient and upset you. I am of course talking about the following unprecedented axiom: **You should buy a filing cabinet** (cue dramatic music).

Though seemingly trivial, the simple act of buying—and using—a filing cabinet can have a big impact on your stress levels and effectiveness as a college student. Really. The idea here is simple. At college, living alone for the first time, you have to deal with a surprising amount of paperwork and important documents. There are housing requests, forms for declaring your major, financial-aid information, event schedules, and bills. Not to mention class-specific information such as syllabi, lecture outlines, and assignment specifications. At first you might be able to get away with the classic collegiate throw-and-search method, where you throw important papers somewhere in the vicinity of your desk, and then, when it comes time to find a specific document, search until you either locate it or deem it unrecoverable. The problem is that once you begin losing important papers, or begin losing large amounts of time clawing through your drawers and notebooks, your stress levels rise unnecessarily. It's human nature: to have lost something important unsettles us. We like to know where things are.

There is enough unavoidable stress at college that you shouldn't have to deal with this problem. So buy a filing cabinet. Or at the very least, get one of those simple plastic boxes that hold hanging file folders, or grab a cheap plastic crate that can serve the same purpose. Always have a large supply of hanging file folders and labels readily available. Then, whenever you come across a piece of paper that you need to hold on to, either put it in an existing folder or, if no relevant category exists, take thirty seconds to label a new folder to hold it. This is the easiest form of filing, it takes very little time to accomplish, and it works. There is a bit of a thrill connected with being able to get your fingers on any piece of information within seconds. You feel like an organizational guru, and it prevents undue frustration.

Using a simple filing system is just plain practical. Worry about the big problems of academic life; don't let organization issues steal too much of your attention or energy.

# 69

**Find a Secret Study Space**

*In Rule #31,* "Don't Study in Your Room," I explain that because there are so many distractions at college, studying in a quiet, somber, distraction-free location such as the library is very important. This is imperative to keep in mind because studying well is hard. It takes a lot of effort to achieve the concentration needed to learn material effectively, and going to the library is a good first step. As mentioned before, your dorm room offers more distractions than the typical Las Vegas casino, and by escaping to somewhere far away and quiet you will be much more productive.

However, there is another twist. For your most serious, arduous, and important studying tasks, it's sometimes not enough to just cruise to any old spot in the library. **You need to find your own secret study space.** A location that you know will almost always be available; a monastic corner where silence is complete,

CAL NEWPORT

Zenlike concentration a given, and all distractions are deflected. The more unusual or unconventional the location the better. For me, my secret study space was a little-used carrel at the end of a dimly lit, nonwindowed book aisle on a random unfurnished floor of the biomedical library (never mind that I wasn't a biomed student, the spot was quiet). Sitting at the end of the dark passage, shelves of books stacked behind and in front of me, a concrete wall hemming me in from the third side, in complete silence, I found that I could work for hours with stunning concentration. If I had instead grabbed a seat at one of the busy tables on the first floor of the main library, my productivity would have been dramatically diminished. Take the time to explore the odd corners and depths of your favorite buildings on campus, and you will certainly find a hidden jewel of a study space to call your own.

The key to making the most out of your secret study space is to use it sparingly. Over time, it becomes depressing to study in such isolation. If you insist on completing every reading assignment, problem set, and short paper in this seclusion, you will soon feel quite lonely. In addition, as any college student will tell you, if you complete too much tedious work in any one given location, you will begin to associate discomfort with that particular spot. You don't want to burn out your hidden study oasis, so use it only for major assignments, midterms, finals, and truly daunting papers. For everything else, switch your location often, and study in well-lit, well-populated areas of the library. This selective use of your secret study space will increase its effectiveness. When the stakes are

173

high, you will have the confidence of knowing that there is a zone of intense concentration ready to provide you with the results you need.

If you can maximize the use of your surroundings, you can maximize your performance as a student.

## 70

## Study with the Quiz-and-Recall Method

*You may have* noticed that the topic of studying occurs quite frequently in this book. We talked about how early to begin studying,
why elaborate study systems are effective, and the advantage of
fifty-minute chunks. We talked about where not to study, who not
to study with, why the library is so important, and how to use a secret study space. However, we have not yet talked about how to actually learn the material once you begin the actual act of studying.

There are many theories about how best to take information
from the page and make it your own. There are whole books de-
voted to the subject, and there are cognitive scientists who have
made careers out of probing the learning process. However, if you
are looking for a solution that is time-tested, that works consistently for some of the country's most successful students, you need
look no further than the quiz-and-recall method. The details of this

approach are simple. For any material you have to learn, be it complicated social science theories, foreign language verb conjugations, or physics equations, your basic study method should always involve quizzing and recalling. I don't mean this lightly. Asking yourself a handful of review questions doesn't count. **You should build your entire approach to studying around the concept that making yourself recall specific information is the absolute best way to learn.**

Take, for example, a political science exam where you will be given essay questions on various theoretical frameworks. As you move through your elaborate study system, begin to draw up a quiz for each theory. The quiz can have basic questions about who was responsible for each theory, when it was published, and what topics it involves. If you covered four major arguments against a particular theory, put down a question along the lines of: "List the four major arguments against Theory X, who is responsible for each, and what flaw they described." Your final study goal is to ace these quizzes without peeking at your notes. Once you can do that, you are ready for the exam.

Take as another example a computer science exam for a class about operating systems. You know your exam will cover both applied questions, where you use techniques learned in class to solve a new problem, and straightforward factual questions. Your study quiz could then consist of questions dealing with all the major fact-based topics, as well as an example problem to solve for each of

176

the major applied techniques you might have to use. Again, once you can ace these quizzes, you are ready to go.

This approach turns studying into a two-step process. The first step is the long and silent review of all the material that is going to be on the test. While you do this review, jot down your recall questions. If you ask about a topic from a specific book, jot down the page number where the answer can be found. If you ask about something from your notes, jot down the date of the relevant lecture. This will save a lot of time when you forget an answer later on.

The next step of the process is the quizzing. This is where the real learning actually happens. When quizzing yourself, you don't necessarily have to write down your answers. This might be necessary for solving math problems, but for discussion-style questions, feel free to formulate your response out loud. You can cover topics much quicker when you just have to talk as opposed to write. However, if speaking out loud, it's important that you still use complete sentences. The more clearly you articulate your thoughts, the more clearly you remember the information.

This technique is remarkably effective because it forces you to recall the information from scratch. The act of pulling the information from your memory and articulating the main points cements knowledge much stronger than just reading it over a couple of times. Reviewing notes on a topic can only take you so far. Your mind is perfectly willing to read the same words hundreds of times without making any real effort to remember them. But if you actually make yourself stare at a blank sheet of paper and recall answers from no other source than your brain, you *will* remember that material. This is guaranteed. Another trick is to involve emotion. Don't just sit at a desk and talk quietly. Stand up, pace your room, yell out answers, cover material as if lecturing to a fascinated class, and play inspiring music in the background. The more stimuli you provide your brain, the more connections to the material you will develop, and the better you will remember and understand it.

In fact, this technique saves you time and provides peace of mind. Your goal for studying is no longer an amorphous promise to "review all the relevant material"; instead, it's the much more specific "review all the relevant material until I can ace all my quizzes." If you can pass your quizzes in two hours, then you are done studying in two hours. If it takes you three days, then you are done studying in three days—but at least at the end you will know you are ready.

The quiz-and-recall method is near miraculous in its ability to consistently provide you with top results. And if you are innovative in your attempts to keep your energy level high while recalling the information, it can even be, dare we say it, *fun*. Whatever else you do to study, never approach an exam without first having made yourself recall all the relevant information from scratch.

## 71

# Empty Your In-Box

*As long as* we are talking about organization, there is an electronic version of disarray that can cause just as much stress as an unkempt room or ineffective filing system. I'm talking about your overflowing e-mail in-box. These days, everyone at college has a computer and a fast network connection, so a lot of communication occurs via e-mail. Some messages are junk, some are snippets of electronic conversations you had with friends, some have sentimental value, and some have important information you need to hold on to. **Organize the messages in your e-mail in-box like you would your paper files.**

Create a separate electronic folder for specific class-related e-mails, family e-mails, and friend e-mails. Also create a generic *important* folder to hold messages containing any random information you need to hang on to. For every e-mail you read, either trash it or file it. At the end of each day you should go to sleep with an empty e-mail in-box.

Again, this isn't rocket science, but it will make you feel a little less stressed, a little more organized, and therefore energized. And the bigger point here is not the rule itself but the mind-set it promotes. Many of these rituals of small-scale organization offer a large-scale sense of control. And this mind-set is necessary for success.

So, treat your e-mail in-box like you do the rest of your life, with an eye toward organization, ease, and efficiency.

# 72

**Relax Before Sleep**

*Throughout this book* we have discussed your body as if you are try-

ing to extract maximum performance from a demanding machine.
We talked about consistently sleeping the right number of hours,
eating the proper food, exercising, and avoiding the naps and all-
nighters that destroy your sleep cycle. Now it's time for a body-
related rule that won't make you cringe: **Relax for at least half
an hour before you go to sleep.**

When you schedule each day you should always indicate a
cutoff point when you will stop all work. On a light day, early in a
semester or right after exams, this cutoff may be relatively early in
the evening. Which is great, go out and enjoy! But during the inevitable busy stretches, you will always have more work than you
can accomplish on any given day, so for your own well-being you
have to impose a deadline on your daily chaos. For me, during fi-

nals and midterms, this cutoff was usually around eleven P.M., but the specific time really depends on the urgency of your workload and when you typically go to bed.

Here is what's important: after you pass your daily work cutoff point, never move right into sleep. If you go to bed with the stresses of the day fresh on your mind, you will have a harder time falling asleep, and psychologically you deny your mind the chance to recover from the pressures of the day. Instead, you should always relax for at least half an hour before going to sleep. Watch a TV show, read, play your guitar, talk to a friend. It doesn't matter what you do, as long as it doesn't involve any schoolwork and it makes you happy. Furthermore, really make an effort during this time to completely block out thoughts about upcoming obligations or work deadlines. Some of the happiest and most successful students I have ever met possess an almost superhuman ability to shut off stressful thoughts once they decide they are done for the day. This is a practiced skill, one you should work on.

When you consistently fall asleep relaxed, you sleep better, you are happier, and you have more energy the next day. The work lost to your nighttime relaxation will be more than compensated for by your refreshed spirit the next morning.

# 73

## Start Fast, End Slow

*The typical student* strategy for writing a paper, studying for a test, researching a project, completing an application, or working on any other big assignment is to figure out the absolute latest point at which they can start working and still finish by the deadline. The generic way of describing this approach is to start slow, end fast. You probably recognize the downsides of having such a stressful philosophy. It basically ensures that you maximize the amount of frantic rushing involved with every assignment you work on. A lot of students unwittingly follow this approach, and this is why so many of them burn out at college. Fortunately, there are alternatives. In this book, we have described several specific strategies for countering this problematic philosophy. There was Rule #4, "Start Long-Term Projects the Day They Are Assigned"; Rule #26, "Start Studying Two Weeks in Advance"; and Rule #41, "Use Three Days to Write a Paper." But this mind-set is so ingrained in students, and so damaging, it warrants a rule of its own. **To be a successful student, you must abandon the start-slow, end-fast mind-set, and instead approach all projects by aiming to start fast, end slow.** It's a subtle variation, but it makes a big difference.

Take, for example, a funding proposal for a club you run. If you have two weeks to finish it, plan to have most of it done by the end of the first week. The day before you leave for spring vacation, do your packing in the morning, not late at night. If you have a big class presentation to research, complete the work with days to spare. No matter how big or how small the assignment, get in the habit of starting fast and ending slow. if you make a point of getting as much accomplished as early as possible, your life will be significantly less frantic. This is a fundamental shift in how most students approach their work, but if you give it a try, you will become much more successful.

# 74

## Spend a Semester Studying Abroad

*Have you ever* enjoyed a cup of morning coffee while watching the
sun rise over the Parisian cityscape? Have you ever spent a lazy afternoon in the shadow of St. Peter's Basilica in Rome? Have you
ever wandered the streets of Prague, content to just take in the foreign ambience? Imagine having experiences like these every day
for three months or more. Imagine how beneficial it would be for
you to explore the world while you are still young, to take in other
cultures, to learn a new language, to get a huge new sense of perspective on your life. There is an easy way to make all of this a reality: **Spend a semester studying abroad.**

Almost every college has study abroad programs. Some are
language-focused, where you live with a family and try to build flu-
ency in their native language through cultural immersion. Others
are focused on specific academic concentrations, like art history,

where students can travel to Florence to study Italian renaissance art and architecture. And it's not just liberal arts majors who go on these trips. It's not uncommon for an Earth science program to sponsor a term in Africa, or a biology program to send students to the Galapagos Islands. In short, there is a study abroad opportunity for basically any student who is interested. *You* should be interested.

There are many benefits to going abroad. To start with, never again in your life will it be this easy to spend so much time overseas. The school takes care of all the details. The money is handled as part of your tuition, and you're getting course credit, so you're not sacrificing anything to make the experience possible. It's a sad but true fact that unless you become independently wealthy, there will be few opportunities later in life to drop everything and spend a whole season exploring a foreign country.

While there, you will also have the life-changing experience of truly coming to understand another culture. This global perspective will inform every aspect of your life, from the way you read a newspaper to the way you shape your career to your views on American politics. You will also most likely pick up a second language, which looks good on your résumé and is a wonderful skill that you can use for years to come. And most important, going abroad is a fun and exciting thing to do that will make you a more interesting, multifaceted person. Why not take advantage of such an opportunity?

There is, however, one caveat: you have to choose the right program. Most schools have two types of foreign study programs:

fluff programs and serious ones. The fluff programs typically involve the Americans skipping classes, drinking like it's their job, socializing only with one another, and in general experiencing very little of the actual culture. The serious programs, on the other hand, are structured in such a way as to encourage the students to actually befriend foreigners, spend time away from the group, enhance language skills, continue with substantial academics, and create an authentic overall experience. So when you decide which programs to apply for, talk to students who have already been on the trips. This is the best way to ascertain the true character of a particular program. There's a big difference between studying English literature at Oxford and heading to Germany for three months of pub crawling.

Also keep in mind that applications for studying abroad are usually due sometime during your sophomore year. They also typically require that you take certain prerequisite courses before you apply, so you should start looking into this opportunity early in your collegiate career to make sure you are prepared.

Studying abroad is a once-in-a-lifetime experience. Don't let it pass you by.

# 75

## "Don't Have No Regrets"

*When interviewing people* for this book, I came across one student in particular who seemed to possess a wonderful sense of contentment. He was of course extraordinarily accomplished, but his happiness did not stem from specific achievements. He seemed to be immune to the pressures or stresses of becoming a top-tier student. Intrigued, I pushed him to reveal more about his philosophy on life, the root of his contentment. And he finally rewarded me with a simple piece of advice: **"Don't have no regrets."** This sage quip had been passed to him by a family friend whom he greatly admired, and he had taken the words to heart.

To not have "no regrets" is to approach life with a sense of excitement and possibility. It's to be happy about your opportunities, not your successes. The fact that you are able to have the experience of going for a major award, pursuing an interesting research project, or starting a student organization is a great affirmation of your zest for life. If you fail, why waste time with regrets? Be thankful for the experience and ask what's next?

I conclude this book with these words because I believe that pursuing your ambitions for the right reasons is more important than any specific strategy for succeeding at college. If you want to succeed because you like the attention, then this book can't help you. If you want succeed to prove yourself to others, then this book can't help you. If you want to succeed because you enjoy adulation and praise, then this book can't help you. You will never really win, because the fear of failure will always be lurking around the next corner.

If, however, you want to succeed because you love the excitement of pushing your potential and exploring your world and new experiences, if you want to succeed because life is short and why not fill it with as much activity as possible, then you *will* win. If you approach life with an attitude of never having regrets and always having a hopeful smile on your face, you can find a measure of success in all your endeavors. Don't have no regrets, but have plenty of fun along the way. In the end, that is what it is to really win.

# Acknowledgments

I would like to thank all the extraordinary students who helped inspire the rules featured in this book. Their insights made this project possible. I would also like to thank my amazing agent, Laurie
Abkemeier, for her extraordinary efforts in getting this idea from
the proverbial drawing board to the printed page, and my tireless
editor, Ann Campbell, who helped me find my voice and successfully transfer into words the deep passion I feel for this topic.

## About the Author

Beltrami Studios

Cal Newport graduated summa cum laude from Dartmouth College and is currently pursuing a Ph.D. in computer science at the Massachusetts Institute of Technology. His writing on college life and student success has appeared in *College Bound Magazine, Business Today* magazine, the New York Daily News Online, *The Wall Street Journal's College Journal,* StudentLeader.com, NationalLampoon.com, Student.com, and Vault.com.

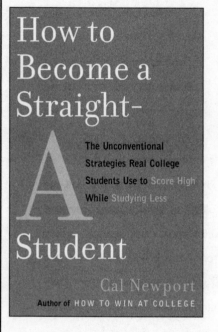

## Also by Cal Newport

### How to Become a Straight-A Student

The Unconventional Strategies
Real College Students Use to
Score High While Studying Less
$13.99 paper (Canada: $17.99)
978-0-7679-2271-5

## Jumpstart your GPA!

A breakthrough approach to acing academic assignments—from
quizzes and exams to essays and papers—*How to Become a
Straight-A Student* reveals for the first time the proven study
secrets of real straight-A students across the country and weaves
them into a simple, practical system that anyone can master.

### How to Be a High School Superstar

A Revolutionary Plan to Get
into College by Standing Out
(Without Burning Out)
$12.99 paper (Canada: $14.99)
978-0-7679-3258-5

# Get into the college of your dreams!

Based on in-depth research and extensive enthusiastic feedback
from the readers of Cal Newport's award-winning student advice
blog, *How to Be a High School Superstar* reveals the seemingly
paradoxical secret to getting into your dream college without
breaking a sweat.